SLIDE SPIN

Your Power of Expression

Essential presentation skills for
career success

notionpress
.com

SLIDE SPIN

Your Power of Expression

Essential presentation skills for career success

Subbarao Mukkavilli

notionpress.com

Notion Press

Old No. 38, New No. 6
McNichols Road, Chetpet
Chennai - 600 031

First Published by Notion Press 2015

ISBN 978-93-84878-82-5

A special gift is waiting for you

Thank you for your interest in my book. I invite you to join the slide spinner club and get a HD presentation template FREE. It is trendy and ready to use.

Visit www.SlideSpinners.Com/Club

Bonus : I will also mail you the editable version of activities and worksheets used in this book

To my family, with love

TABLE OF CONTENTS

READER REVIEWS

The moment we are asked to give a presentation or a sales pitch, the nerves kick in and every negative feeling we've ever had about doing a presentation suddenly tries to take over. Thanks to Subbarao Mukkavilli and Slide Spin: Your Power of Expression, you can calm your fears and create a presentation with confidence. This guide begins by debunking the myths that many of us have concerning our ability to create presentations. Subbarao doesn't stop there, however, he continues to boost confidence by giving us easy to remember and use tools for planning, organizing and perfecting our presentation. Making use of two acronyms, PRISM and SIMPLE, the reader is able to home in on exactly how to develop each slide for the presentation. With an in-depth look at how to not only develop, but distribute your presentation in different formats, Subbarao provides all of the necessary tools to calm your fears and help you create a kick-ass presentation.

Although I'm no stranger to making use of PowerPoint to create video and slide presentations, Slide Spin: Your Power of Expression was extremely helpful for enhancing my perspective on how to get the most bang out of each of my slides. Subbarao Mukkavilli does a great job of not only showing how to create each slide, but provides tools for planning and making certain that each slide and the presentation as a whole is well organized. Believe it or not, you too can create effective presentations. In spite of every objection you might have, Slide Spin: Your Power of Expression and Subbarao's confidence building approach can overcome those objections, fears and self-limitations. It is a must-read for anyone who is in marketing and sales, but goes well beyond those areas as well.

- Bill Howard | Readers Favorite

Slide Spin: Your Power of Expression - Essential presentation development skills for non designers is a business/education text written by Subbarao Mukkavilli. The author introduces the concepts of presentation for business by presenting parallel instances from the personal realm. His character has been awarded a promotion and is planning a celebratory affair -- how does he plan for it? Using PowerPoint, Mukkavilli demonstrates how even those who've never thought of themselves as creative can foster that ability and produce compelling and effective presentations. He explains why presentations are so crucially important; discusses what makes a presentation work; and gives an overview of the online resources that are available and their uses. His appendices include a presentation checklist, links for online resources and tools, and an index.

Subbarao Mukkavilli's educational business text, Slide Spin: Your Power of Expression, is informative and it entertains as it teaches. The author's goal is to show those who've not had formal graphics training how a professional slide presentation can be developed following his guidelines and examples, and he does so brilliantly. I enjoyed seeing how he uses real-life examples to make the concepts he's presenting easily accessible to the reader, and was quite impressed by the presentation he conjures up before the reader's eyes. Mukkavilli's writing style is breezy and casual, and his text is filled with illustrations, anecdotes and inspirational quotes. He succeeds in presenting what could seem to be a complex and somewhat daunting subject in a way that's professional, inspirational and, ultimately, doable. His discussion of the online graphic choices, cloud storage and other online tools presentation designers have at their disposal is thorough and well-presented, and I'm planning on checking out many of the links he shares. Slide Spin: Your Power of Expression is most highly recommended.

- Jack Magnus for Readers' Favorite

Slide Spin: Your Power of Expression by Subbarao Mukkavilli is an engaging 'how to' guide for anyone who has to create a presentation. Divided into three sections, the book focuses on acquiring the tools and techniques necessary to express communication. Using the PRISM framework and SIMPLE checklist, learn the guiding factors for content development and stay on track with your main objective. Articulate new ideas or sell innovative products to gain a competitive edge using persuasive presentations in a methodical method. Explore the rationale behind creating compelling presentations, core concepts, online tools and trends while dispelling myths about creative people. Mukkavilli defines content versus context, the breakdown of graphics programs such as Microsoft PowerPoint, multimedia, distribution, web development, the cloud, talent mining and slide presentations. Supported by case studies, research and experience, Mukkavilli examines structured presentation development and the suitable deployment options.

Slide Spin: Your Power of Expression by Subbarao Mukkavilli is a great way to unleash creative power and make any passion a profession. At the beginning of each of the twelve chapters is a quote from famous people that sums up philosophies on communication. This detailed book is for anyone, not just graphics artists. It guides the reader through the various steps to design a visual presentation. Being a graphic artist myself, I often take for granted the skills I have. I forget that my co-workers may not have the abilities to whip up a slide presentation. This manual is for those people who want a systematic approach in layman's terms.

- Suzanne Cowles

Slide Spin: Your Power of Expression by Subbarao Mukkavilli is a useful guide to those readers who want to unveil the tools of aestheticism and creativity while expressing their ideas and concepts. The book gives readers the confidence to create a successful presentation, shattering the myth that one needs to be a graphic designer, a multimedia expert or artistically inclined to create a presentation. The author gives a lot of useful tips and suggestions to improve on presentations. The book also introduces readers to the two concepts of Prism and Simple, and how helpful they are when it comes to creating a good presentation.

I found the book very useful. The author's suggestions and advice are not complicated and can be tried out by anyone. The style of writing is casual and it reaches out to those who know how to do a presentation and to those who do not. A lot of common myths regarding presentations are demystified through the book. The common myths about presentations and all details about creating a good presentation are discussed in detail, making readers more confident when it comes to creating a good presentation. The section of the book which speaks about corporate presentation gives more insights into how to make a perfect and impressive presentation. The book will also help one to discover their hidden talents and creativity through creating some impressive presentations.

- Mamta Madhavan | Readers' Favorite

Slide Spin: Your Power of Expression by Subbarao Mukkavilli is a great, all-in-one book on the art and craft of creating memorable presentations. Slide Spin: Your Power of Expression explores all of the facets involved in creating and designing presentations in such a way that the message is conveyed in a succinct, impressive, and interesting manner. In Slide Spin, Subbarao Mukkavilli explains how to present information in a way that stands out while making artful use of fonts, colors, images, and glyphs in addition to words. He describes several tips and techniques on how to create designs and presentation slides, and provides links to various useful websites for this purpose. Subbarao Mukkavilli also introduces PRISM and SIMPLE: PRISM is a practical framework for creating presentations, to create the best output with the power to engage the audience, and SIMPLE is a simple checklist that lists the guiding factors for content development for presentations.

Slide Spin: Your Power of Expression by Subbarao Mukkavilli is written in a wonderfully engaging way that feels positive and encouraging at the same time. Subbarao Mukkavilli has provided some examples of presentation slides in this book and I was surprised and impressed at how good they look. This is a very useful book to have for people who give presentations frequently. I also think this book may be useful, even if one does not have to give presentations, because it contains a lot of tips on how to engage with and communicate with people, which can be extended into daily life as well.

- Gisela Dixon for Readers' Favorite

PREFACE

> "If all my possessions were taken from me with one exception, I would choose to keep the power of communication, for by it I would soon regain all the rest."
>
> - Daniel Webster

One of the distinct features of a Democracy is the Freedom of Expression. Similarly, the distinct feature of a Meritocracy is the Power of Expression. While a democracy offers you the freedom of expression, you need to acquire the power of expression in a meritocracy. Slide Spin is all about acquiring such power.

I wrote the book 'Slide Spin' with a lot of passion. I wanted to unveil the tools and techniques involved in achieving the power of expression.

There is a misconception that only graphic designers or those who have good knowledge of creating complex graphics can develop presentations. This myth scares many good people and discourages them.

When you finish reading this book, you will realize that you don't need to be a graphic designer or multimedia expert to create a presentation.

To help you understand this concept, I have introduced a practical framework called 'PRISM' for creating presentations. When you use the PRISM framework to build your presentation, you will be able to create the finest output with the power to engage your audience.

I have also introduced a simple checklist called 'SIMPLE'. This checklist gives you the guiding factors for content development for presentations. The checklist also keeps you on track with respect to our main objective.

As you know, we need to find answers to six questions to find a practical solution to any problem. Those are What, Who, Where, When, Why and How?

I have answered the Why, What, Where and How parts of the question. **You** *need to answer the 'When' part of the question. You will get your answer as soon as you read this book.*

Good luck!

ACKNOWLEDGEMENT

"No duty is more urgent than that of returning thanks".

— *Unknown*

At the outset, I would like to thank my wife Ms. Annapurna for standing by me throughout my career and helping me to become an Author.

I also thank my tiny twin children Vishnu and Karthika for sparing me and allowing me to steal the time I am supposed to give them.

I am also thankful to my parents and brother for their constant support and encouragement throughout my journey.

I am grately indebted to my boss and mentor Mr.C.Parthasarathy - Chairman, Karvy Group. He has gifted me with the Knowledge, Stature and several other prized possessions of mine. This book would not have been possible without his encouragement and support.

I am grateful to Mr.V.Ganesh – CEO, Karvy Computershare Pvt Ltd for providing various opportunities and helping me build the skills I have today.

I am also thankful to Ms.Annette Kolff for spotting the talent in me way back during 1997 and encouraging me to develop the presentation skills.

I would also thank my friend Sridhar Kakarala for his constant help and feedback on the book. I would have given up as a lone fighter without him!

I wish to personally thank Ms.Sandhya Sridhar , Chief Editor – NotionPress.Com for helping me constantly in enriching the book and preserving the perspective.

I would not have been able to complete my book without their support and encouragement.

INTRODUCTION

> "Each work has to pass through these stages—ridicule, opposition, and then acceptance. Those who think ahead of theirtime are sure to be misunderstood."
>
> \- Swami Vivekananda

Power of expression

Your boss can articulate your ideas better than you do. That is the reason why he or she is your boss.

In this competitive world, your career growth is directly linked to your ability to articulate new ideas and explain them using compelling presentations. The skill to make a presentation is the most important tool in our survival kit.

In our day-to-day lives, we come across many brilliant people with several bright ideas. They have a burning desire to do something different and useful for themselves and for their co-workers. They make vain attempts to explain the features and benefits of their ideas. Sadly, there are no takers of their fresh thoughts and perspectives. They then commit a 'thoughticide' and bury the idea. May their thought not rest in peace but resurface strongly!

Similarly, there are many young 'solopreneurs' who come up with innovative products and solutions. They bet their careers on building what they believe and making sure that they work. Finally, when it comes to selling their idea or product, they fumble. They find it extremely difficult to express the benefits of their product or invention to the investors or the people who can fund their mission.

We see many people who lose opportunities, skip their salary raise or chances of moving up the ladder.

What is common to these failures?

They fail to tell the story. They fail to unveil the critical factor called WIIFM - What Is In It For Me. They lack the power of expression.

What causes communication failures?

Some people suffer from a condition called **Thought Constipation**. *They have excessive difficulty in articulating and expressing their thoughts in a simple yet 'comprehendible' fashion.*

When they start expressing their thoughts, they encounter another problem called 'Word Salad'. And I assure you, this salad has nothing to do with good health!

Wikipedia describes this condition as follows:

> *Word salad is a "confused or unintelligible mixture of seemingly random words and phrases", most often used to describe a symptom of a neurological or mental disorder. The words may or may not be grammatically correct, but semantically confused to the point that the listener cannot extract any meaning from them.*
>
> *Word salad may describe a symptom of neurological or psychological conditions in which a person attempts to communicate an idea, but words and phrases that may appear to be random and unrelated come out in an incoherent sequence instead. Often, the person is unaware that he or she did not make sense.*

So then, what do we call a presentation created by a person with this condition? ***Slide Salad or Slidorrhea.***

Do you need this book?

This book helps two categories of people.

1. *Those who develop presentations*
2. *Those who do not develop presentations*

No pun intended.

If you are a person who is frequently tasked with creating presentations, you will benefit from the techniques explained in this book. You will be able to develop persuasive presentations in a methodical manner.

If you are someone who has the luxury of delegating this job, you still need to understand and appreciate the critical elements that go into the presentation. Once you understand behind-the-scenes strategy, you will be able to provide better quality inputs to the developer, as also deliver presentations with ease.

Still, not sure? Please try to answer the following questions:

1. *I always struggle to explain my ideas to my friends and colleagues. My boss trashes most of my ideas.*
2. *I want to take a new initiative that can transform my workplace but I don't know how to initiate the discussion.*
3. *The application I use at office really sucks. I have few ideas on improving the user interface but I do not know how to explain it to the IT team.*
4. *We have created a great product but none of our clients/ prospects seem to be interested.*
5. *We have great products and services but our clients and prospects always undervalue them.*
6. *Our prospects stop responding to my calls after I send my presentation to them.*
7. *I know that our presentation looks outdated but I don't have any idea how to improve it.*

8. *I have been making in vain attempts to get the funding but no one seems to be interested.*

If you have answered YES to at least three questions, then this book is for you.

Chances are that you have some bright ideas. When they are articulated well, you can get the buy-in from the key stakeholders, which in turn, can lead to good rewards and recognition. The idea can probably transform your workplace, make you more productive or can get you that funding you are looking for; or that pay hike that you rightfully deserve.

Chances are that you want to create meaningful slides and not slide salads.

If this is true, you are at the right place at the right time. The concepts and ideas explained in this book will certainly empower you with the necessary skills to give you that competitive edge.

This book assumes that you have the working knowledge of any presentation software like PowerPoint, Keynote and/or any other open source equivalent. Since the examples used in this book are created using PowerPoint, this book also assumes that you are familiar with the menu options available in the latest PowerPoint version.

Once you have completed reading this book and understand the concepts explained here, you should be able to express your thoughts better and market yourself with ease.

Sounds great? Let's get started...

Structure of the book

This book is divided into three sections.

The first section explains the rationale behind creating compelling presentations and demystifies various myths behind creating them.

In the second section, we will dive deep into the core concepts of creating effective presentations. The concepts explained in this section are based on a proprietary framework called PRISM.

When a stream of light passes through a prism, the light is transformed into a spectrum of colors. Similarly, we will learn how to transform our presentation into a stream of bright colors when we pass it through the PRISM framework.

To articulate the concepts better and to demonstrate certain practical aspects of presentation creation, I have used the latest windows version of PowerPoint. The techniques explained using PowerPoint can also be used in other popular presentation software like Apple Keynote and certain open office versions.

All PowerPoint examples used in the book are also available online: htttp://slidespinners.com

The third section outlines various concepts, ideas and online tools to further fortify our message.

In this section, we will also explore various new trends in presentation creation.

CHAPTER 1

THE PARTY

> "Either I will find a way or make one."
>
> *- Philip Sidney*

Sam is exuberant. He has been unable to contain his joy and ecstasy since morning.

For Sam has received some excellent news that morning. His boss had called him in at 10AM and had told him that he had been promoted. He has been chosen to run their Centre of Excellence independently.

Sam will receive a 100% hike in salary, with a 13th check worth a full year's salary as performance bonus.

The new role also entitles him to some handsome perks. Overall, this is a great growth curve for him.

Sam is a bright executive in his early 30s. His charming personality and now charming position will make him the most eligible bachelor in the town.

He wants to celebrate his success and wants to host a fabulous party. He also thinks that it is time to announce his marriage with Samantha, early next year.

He has been postponing this celebration for quite sometime now. His close pals constantly complain about this.

So he wants to host a grand party and make it a memorable experience for his guests. He plans a day-long event filled with fun and frolic. He invites all his friends, relatives and acquaintances.

Some of his close pals are Duty-full and Spiritual. They are called Duty-full and Spiritual because they thrive on the best of the spirits/ liqueurs and pay heavy excise tax/duty.

He wants to keep them delighted and therefore has promised them a carton full of a very special and the oldest imported Scotch.

It is the first time that he is hosting a party of this order. Although Sam has finalized an event manager for this, he wants to personally get involved in many areas. So he takes three days off to oversee the arrangements.

He carefully finalizes the guest list, decides the food menu according to what he thinks could be the choice and preferences of his invitees. He selects the return gifts based on the guests' profile.

For a few elders who do not check their email often, he also keeps 'thank you' cards ready.

He finalizes the venue, various events and their sequences.

After a great deal of brainstorming, he finalizes the agenda.

The itinerary

6 AM to 6 PM | Party games, shows and adventure sports

6 PM to 8 PM | Cocktails

8 PM to 10 PM | Dinner

The big day

Finally the day arrives. Most of the people invited for the party turn up on time. A few senior colleagues and clients have also promised to join the cocktail party.

Soon after the welcome drinks, the event manager keeps all guests captivated with a series of outdoor party games. The whole day goes like a song.

Now it is evening and cocktail time. The time our spiritual pals have been waiting for.

Around 5PM, Sam's assistant tells him that he has not received the Scotch cartons because the supplier has messed up the delivery. Sam is furious and disturbed, but he is left with no choice.

He furiously calls up the local bootlegger who is the supplier, and gives him a mouthful. The bootlegger apologizes for the botch-up. He offers to send him cartons of the local brew, free of cost. He also tells Sam that his niece,who is a celebrity, is incidentally in town. She can entertain the guests as a gesture of compensation.

Sam is further upset with all these free offers and suggestion of compensation. He hangs up on the bootlegger. He calls up various other sources, but draws a blank.

He composes himself and tries to think about a Plan-B. He has two options now. One is to continue with what is available. The second is to take some of the guests into confidence and request them for help. This second option is little embarrassing as he knows that his close friends would say that they would manage with what is available. That would be even worse! Sam does not know what to do.

Sensing his turmoil, Samantha approaches Sam to find out what the problem is. Sam tells her about the botch-up and explains that he does not want to disappoint the dutiful and Spiritual gang.

Samantha laughs aloud and tells him that Chris, her father is an accomplished trouble-shooter who could help his Plan B, C, D and whatever else he would want.

Sam calls up Chris and explains the situation. He requests him for help. Chris laughs aloud much like Samantha did and assures him that he would ensure the delivery within half an hour.

This is indeed great relief for Sam! He thanks Samantha for her presence of mind and proceeds to the banquet hall.

Within 30 minutes, the cartons arrive. Sam opens the cartons in anticipation. To his surprise, they are the finest quality available!

He invites the guests to start the cocktails. To his surprise, the bootlegger's niece also arrives by 6 PM.

The sudden appearance of a celebrity instantly turns the party quotient up notches, and the guests get energised.

The celebrity show becomes the highlight of the day!

The celebrity announces Sam and Samantha's imminent wedding before leaving and the next round of cheer starts. The party continues till midnight.

Sam is extremely happy with the party and thanks Samantha for everything.

2 CHAPTER

COMMON MYTHS DEMYSTIFIED

"Talk to yourself at least once in a day. Otherwise you may miss a meeting with an excellent person in this world."

- Swami Vivekananda

Before we embark on our journey, we need to clear certain inhibitions and mental blocks.

First - what is the similarity between a party at home and the prospect of a sales pitch at the workplace?

Actually, everything!

Both need extensive preparation, planning, a fair degree of personalization, expectation-management, event management, excitement creation and sustenance; and most importantly, an extreme attention to detail.

We host events and parties at home. Similarly, we invite prospects for presentations.

We face similar situations for both events, but our reactions are entirely different!

The takeaways

Let's look at Sam's party in detail.

- *For a one-hour party, he took 20x time for preparation*
- *He took utmost care to profile his guests and capture their preferences accurately*
- *He ensured that the food he served had reasonable variety to appeal to everyone's taste buds*
- *He did not leave any important items to chance and did not delegate them to others*
- *He did not hesitate to ask for help when required*
- *He put in every effort to ensure that the event went off as planned and exceeded the expectations of the guests*
- *His attention to detail was at its highest*

Sam's only objective was to exceed the expectations of guests.

Sam is not unique. All of us do the same thing. At home, we TAKE CHARGE!

For a personal event, web or row several qualities:

1. *Eagle's eye*
2. *Cheetah's energy*
3. *Cat's reflexes*
4. *Ant's hard work*
5. *Bee's persistence*

Let's move to a similar event at the workplace. All our good qualities are lent to someone!

Aspect	*Personal event*	*Workplace event*
Time taken for preparation	*20x*	
Effort to understand the guest profile and preferences	*Very deep* *To the last mile*	
Grooming	*High*	
Presentation	*The best*	
Post-event thanksgiving	*Very courteous*	

To summarize, we are indeed endowed with all the required qualities and abilities, but the display of leadership and usage of skills are purely situational and conditional.

When it comes to creating presentations at workplace, we often tend to undermine our capabilities.

Common myths about presentations

- *Myth#1: I am not a creative person.*
- *Myth#2: My current job does not demand presentation skills.*
- *Myth # 3: We have very good content on our website, plenty of advertisement material designed by our ad agency. We also have the latest research reports. I can include all these in my presentation.*
- *Myth # 4: We have very good content on our website. I just need to copy and paste the content in to my presentation and I am done.*
- *Myth # 5: I am part of a small team with no expertise in design or marketing skills. It is not possible to produce a great output.*

- *Myth #6: Creating presentations is a daunting task. I don't have an expert at presentations to help me when I am struck. Why start something that I cannot complete anyway?*
- *Myth #7: I have seen some of the best presentations with awesome graphics, animations and brilliant presentation techniques. I don't understand graphic design; I know nothing about creative tools.*

Myth#1: I am not a creative person.

What is creativity? It is all about questioning the basics and breaking the traditional rules of thinking. It is about finding a new angle or bringing a fresh perspective.

*Creativity is neither a gift that acquired by birth or a legacy that can be inherited. Creativity is not a super-specialty like Rocket Design or Neurosurgery. We have heard people say, "***Born with a silver spoon in the mouth***" but have we ever heard anyone say, "***Born with a streak of creativity in the brain***."?*

It is a skill that you can develop and nurture any time, irrespective of your age, gender or class. By doing some simple mental conditioning, we can become creative enough to design a high quality presentation.

If you have written a leave letter in the past and have managed to get a week off, then you are creative enough! We will build from there.

How can a simple leave letter demonstrate your presentation abilities?

Let's look at how:

- *You want a week off.*
- *You know that your boss will get upset if you ask for a break.*
- *However, it is extremely critical that you get it.*
- *There is a desire. There is a compulsion.*
- *You can clearly visualize the consequence of both success and failure.*
- *You will be ready with responses to the FAQs that will follow.*
- *You will gauge the mood of your boss.*
- *You will find the correct time to meet your boss.*
- *You broach the topic, present the case and probably give him a commitment in return.*
- *Finally you convince him!*

All of this might happen in less than an hour, but the episode does not lack spice and entertainment!

Now, you explain this episode to your colleagues. They listen to this, theirs slack jawed.

Now we have a strong story as well. There is a hero, a villain, a mission and a happy ending. Most importantly, a captivated audience!

That's all that is required to build a powerful presentation. In fact, this story is powerful enough to qualify for the script of a block-buster movie. If this story is given to the right director, we can expect to see a 1,000 episode TV soap opera!

Let's sum it up now:

- *Creativity is present in every human mind.*
- *However, it may be in 'sleeping mode' in some people.*
- *But it will surely emerge when awakened.*

Myth#2: My current job does not demand presentation skills.

Many people feel that presentation skills are needed only for sales or marketing personnel. It's like saying, "I don't need to have dress-sense because I am not a model or a film actor/actress."

The need for effective presentation skills is ever growing. This is no longer in the optional/desired category. We need these skills to get into a new position or retain your current one.

In most cases, acquiring presentation skills is like passing through graduation. Graduation on its own may not have value, but not becoming a graduate will certainly haunt you for the rest of the life. If you are not sure, ask any non-graduate and you will get your answer.

Look at the impact of the following scenarios. Look at the positive and negative impacts created by the presence of/absence of presentation skills.

1. *Selling your ideas to the team*
2. *Giving the required comfort to your boss/client as to what is expected from you and your team*
3. *Saving precious time, energy and money that could be lost in communication gaps*
4. *Getting you the next pay hike or promotion*

You will notice that all the above activities project your credibility, professionalism and your relationships within the team. It also reflects your personal growth and the growth of the people reporting to you.

Myth # 3: We have very good content on our website, plenty of advertisement material designed by our ad agency. We also have the latest research reports. I can include all these in my presentation.

Good luck! If all of these are readily available, why waste time on a presentation? Why can't we send these on and close the deal over a telephone call?

Of course, we know that it does not work that way.

Many companies spend millions in revenue on print and media advertisements, TV commercials and online ad campaigns to attract prospective clients or investors. Finally, when a hot prospect is ready to give them an hour, they get confused and end up confusing the client. Result? A happy competitor.

The messages designed for print and media ads have a reasonable life. They get multiple chances of being seen. If someone does not understand the message on the first day, he will understand it on the 100th day.

Your final pitch to a prospect is much like playing a match final. You have reached this stage after clearing several rounds and you need to get this final leg right at any cost. So, the presentation you make at this juncture will only be seen once. You may not get another opportunity to impress the prospect.

Myth # 4: We have very good content on our website. With a simple copy and paste, I am done.

In many ways, presentation development and website development are similar.

- *They follow a structured development life cycle*
- *They thrive on good content*
- *They need strong architecture and design before they are created (coding for a website or slide creation in presentations)*
- *The slides or pages need to follow a structured and logical path*
- *They need to be visually appealing*
- *They get only the shortest possible time to impress*

- *They need to take care of security, privacy and confidentiality aspects*
- *They need to be designed so they can be viewed on multiple devices and resolutions*
- *Finally, their potential is largely misunderstood and frequently ignored by business development personnel*

We should certainly try to adapt the best practices of website development for presentation development.

However, the content and presentation techniques should be more polished and precise in presentations. Why? Because it is the final attempt before we clinch the deal.

Myth # 5: I am part of a small team with no expertise in design or marketing skills. It is not possible to produce a great output.

Let's consider the case of a large organization. This organization has a large manufacturing unit and a large distribution network. A team of engineers drive the production. The finished goods are sold by their sales and marketing team using their distribution network. Their marketing team constantly whets the consumer appetite with various initiatives like advertisements, promotions and so on.

It is feasible for large organizations to have multiple teams that fulfil various functions and responsibilities.

Now, think of yourself as an organization. One part of your brain is the manufacturing unit. You need to build another unit for thought-distribution.

Assuming that you have the manufacturing unit to produce ideas, this book shows you how to build a strong thought-distribution network. Once you become aware of building the thought-

distribution network, you can even distribute thoughts that have been 'manufactured' by others.

Myth #6: Creating presentations is a daunting task. I don't have an expert at presentations to help me when I am struck. Why start something that I cannot complete anyway?

Agreed. Creating a persuasive presentation is a tough task. However, with the right mindset, the right tools and a structured path, we can simplify the task to a great extent. With a little effort, we can also develop our skills at creating presentations.

In chapter 12, we will look at various ways of exploring and nurturing our creativity, as also discover various online resources to help us do this.

Myth #7: I have seen some of the best presentations with awesome graphics, animations and brilliant presentation techniques. I don't understand graphic design; I know nothing about creative tools.

Welcome to Slide Spin again.

This is the biggest myth that we are going to bust.

In general, most people get intimidated by technical jargons on graphic design. They are forced to believe that they need a specialized diploma or even a doctorate in graphic/creative designing to be able to produce a presentation. The answer is 'No'.

There is popular belief that presentations are all about managing design elements with colors, fonts and graphics. These are no doubt important but what is more important is the underlying strength of the message.

Before we think about these elements, we need to get the core structural elements right.

Think of your presentation as a model getting ready for a fashion show.

We need to build the frame or skeleton properly. We also need to make sure that the skin shows good texture. We can dress this up suitably and apply make-up as required, to enhance the overall look. Contrary to this, if we build a structure that does not look human and the skin-texture for instance, resembles that of a tree or an animal, then dressing it up and applying make-up will only result in a disaster. The overall appearance will be that of a zombie or something equally horrendous.

People would have told you that you need to have a good sense of color, font, etc. to create good slides.These are important but only after you get the content right.

Only products with balanced design and engineering will look and feel good. Presentations are no exception. You need the right blend of Design (aesthetics, visual appeal) and Engineering (content, appropriate statements that highlight the client's problem and the benefits of using the product).

The next 10 chapters are all about creating visually appealing presentations that convey the right messages.

In the next section, we are going to look at how we can develop a practical framework to show case our ideas and produce something which will help get our point across.

CHAPTER 3

A COLORFUL WORLD

> "All great undertakings of the world are achieved through mighty obstacles."
>
> \- *Swami Vivekananda*

Your prospect is searching for something. He has a faint idea that the solution he is searching for may be available in a different city.

To get to the new city, he has to travel through a tunnel. However, he does not know the length of the tunnel. He does not even know if this is the right tunnel that will lead to his goal. He does not know how much time it will take to travel through it. He decides to take a chance and walks into the tunnel. It is completely dark. There is no clarity. He is hopeful of finding someone who can give him directions. Relieve him of the uncertainty once and for all.

At the other end, the tunnel forks into two. Each path leads to different cities. One is your city and the other is your competitors'. You are at this other end and you need to walk to your client and show him the path. You need to make sure that you are faster in reaching your client than your competitor is.

To guide your prospect better, you need to take a powerful searchlight with you. You know that your competitor will also carry a similar light, perhaps one more powerful than yours. So, the chances are that the prospect may gravitate to your competitor.

So, you need to make it different. Your light should be brighter. Brighter at least, than the one that your competitor is carrying. Ideally, this should also beam a spectrum of multiple colors. It should act as a beacon to the prospect and draw him to you. Then it is easy for you to understand his requirements better so that you can work towards providing him the most appropriate solutions.

Welcome to **PRISM.**

In this section, we are going to look at a framework that puts structure to our thoughts and helps us prepare a presentation that our prospects are longing to see.

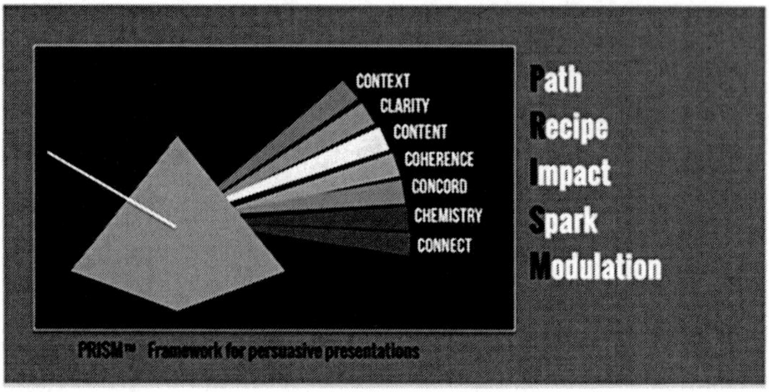

Our thoughts are like a beam of white light. When we pass it through this framework, we get seven different colors.

1. *Context*
2. *Clarity*
3. *Content*
4. *Coherence*
5. *Concord*

6. *Chemistry*
7. *Connect*

Let's see how we can get PRISM to emit these.

☑ *Path*

☑ *Recipe*

☑ *Impact*

☑ *Spark*

☑ *Modulation*

The next five chapters will describe the framework and format in detail.

Rule: Your presentations are accountable for your success.

Fact: Presentations always silently deliver what they are accountable for.

Now the question is: Whom are they working for?

- *You*
- *Your competitor*

Your Spin Strategy in the presentation answers this question.

> *A ball in cricket or baseball delivers results either for you or your opponent. A slow-paced, direct and predictable ball delivers results to your opponent. A fast-paced ball with the right spin will surely stump your opponent.*
>
> *Presentation slides also work on the same principle.*

We will look at the spin strategies and techniques in the next section.

Section 2

PRISM

CHAPTER 4

THE PATH TO VICTORY

> "The will to win is important. But the will to prepare is vital."
>
> *- Joe Paterno*

In this section, we will establish the objective of your presentation and what it seeks to accomplish. We will then find the quickest path to this goal. We will ensure that the path is the one with the least resistance and the highest receptivity.

We will start the process by visualizing the big picture. It is extremely important for us to set the correct context before starting the journey.

Let's assume you are presenting your credentials to a CEO. What should be the ideal content and the slide sequence? There are no set formulae. It varies.

If the CEO is part of a jury evaluating the business potential and you are one among the many contenders, you need to start with a brief explanation about your company and its offerings. You can then move on to other Unique Selling Propositions, as well as the potential that your product has.

If the same CEO is doing a final evaluation of your product or service before hiring you, you need not start with introducing your company. In this scenario, it is most probable that you would have responded to their RFP/Bid and that he or she is reasonably aware of what your organization stands for. Your ability and willingness to handle the assignment may be *under test here.*

In the cases mentioned above, while the presenter and the audience are the same, the context of the presentations will vary.

When it comes to presentations,'**Content is the king and Context is the Kingpin.'**

So, it is important to consider the intent and the objective of the presentation before we plunge into the creation of the slides.

We need to answer the following questions before creating every presentation.

1. *What are the stakes?*
2. *What is the delegate/participant profile?*
3. *What is the path that they are most likely to take?*
4. *What is the path that we want them to take? Are we on the same page with them?*
5. *Do we have that AAA (Triple A) rated person in the group?*
6. *What are questions that we need to ask them?*
7. *What do we expect from them towards the end of the journey?*

In this chapter we will cover the path-setting process for a corporate presentation. Although the examples used are more aligned towards a B2B scenario, the concepts are globally applicable for all types of presentations. If you have an idea /a product / a solution and you want to sell the same for recognition/ reward / revenue, you will benefit the most.

So, to illustrate the concept better, we will take the example of Sam's organization.

> *Sam's division has recently developed a document and workflow management solution. It is a crowded market with a number of established players.*
>
> *Many of their competitors are bundling the solution with hardware and some of them are making it even more attractive by offering decent discounts, flexible payment methods and so on.*
>
> *Sam is now pitching to a Fortune 500 company to implement their solution. It is a multi-million dollar deal and Sam has been working for the last six months, responding to their bid invitation and in the process, has created a detailed solution document of over a 1,000 pages.*
>
> *Sam has received a mail that the core project team would be visiting their office next week to get a final solution walk-through. The project SPOC has told him that it is a final stage in the bid process and they will be selecting one solution provider from among three short listed companies.*

This is the most appropriate time to have a brainstorming with all the stakeholders and get all of them on the same page.

This is the stage where we plan with the end in mind.

The first step in the journey is to visualize the benefits of the prospect giving the mandate. It could trigger a press release, a grand gala victory party, etc. This visualization will not only trigger the motivation but will also help every member realize the importance of focusing on the final pitch.

1. What are the stakes?

This is by far the most important question. This question determines what you will win and what you are likely to lose, depending on whether the final pitch is successful or not.

The higher the stakes, the greater the number of hours of preparation, involving more team members.

In this case, it is a prestigious multi-million dollar project with a Fortune 500 client. Success would mean a very good head start for the entire vertical and failure would mean that several heads will roll. Sam's head included!

Although there is no scientific basis for what I am saying, you need to factor in at least one hour for the preparation of each slide.

If you are planning to show 30 slides, you need approximately 30 hours of preparation time.

This is irrespective of the content that is readily available.

2. *What is the delegate/participant profile?*

By looking at the participants' designations/roles, we will be able to guess their intent and answer the following questions.

Irrespective of the occasion of our presentation, it is best to fill the delegate profile sheet.

Sample delegate profile sheet

Network Strength: Member in our team who knows him/her best from the past.

Knowledge: His/her knowledge about the product, service or subject area.

Perception: Past experience with our product or service. Past association with the organization.

The delegate profile sheet gives us very good insights into the team profile of the visitors, and their expectations from the meeting.

3. *What is the path that they are most likely to take?*

This is probably the best time to re-look at the client's problem statement and match what's on it with our delivery items. This should give us the list of reasons why they would want to talk to us.

What are the top five things that they expect from us?

For a business pitch, it is the capability to showcase. For a seminar, it is the subject knowledge or the networking opportunity.

What are the top five things that appealed to them?

S. No	*Person*	*Category*	*Knowledge*	*Perception*	*Specific Expectations*	*Network Strength*
1		*AAA rated person*				
2		*Opinion-maker*				
3		*Trouble-maker/ Troubled party*				
4		*Favorable/ Most inclined*				
5		*Fence-sitter*				
6		*Neutral*				
7		*Unknown*				

- *Product/Service features and USPs (to be listed separately)*
- *Pricing*
- *Post-sale service*
- *Domain Expertise*
- *Brand and Trustworthiness*
- *Security, Privacy and Confidentiality*
- *Service/Product Continuity and road map*
- *Executive Subscription*
- *Best Fit to their current requirements*
- *Other reasons*
- *All of the above*
- *None of the above*

What is the time frame for the presentation?

- *Full day*
- *Half a day*
- *A few hours*

What do they want to see?

- *Presentation*
- *Product demo*
- *Production/Shop-floor walkthrough*
- *Deep Dive Product walkthrough*
- *All of the above*

What is the structure of the presentation?

- *All participants sequentially going through everything*
- *Respective stakeholders / SMEs branching out to see what is most relevant for them*

Who are the participants?

- *CEO / Decision-maker*
- *CXOs*
- *SMEs/ External Consultants/Function heads*

Prepare a SWOT analysis or list the Unique Selling Propositions of the organization.

Assimilate similar facts pertaining to the nearest or short listed competitors.

4. What is the path that we want them to take? Are we on the same page with them?

The above questions serve to give us clarity on client expectations. The next step is to match our showcase theme with their expectations.

In case there is a mismatch or deviation, it is best to set the expectations right by communicating with the primary driver of the project. This is usually the SPOC (Single Point Of Contact) of the prospect organization.

5. Do we have that AAA (Triple A) rated person in the group?

While making investments, we look for the rating of the stock/bond and will make sure that it has the highest rating ie AAA.

Similarly, we also need to deal with the person who carries the AAA (Triple A) rating.

The person who has the following attributes is THE person:

- *Appetite*
- *Affordability*
- *Authority*

This person may or may not have the need but if he/she has the appetite for our solution, it is sufficient for making our pitch.

Similarly, if there is affordability and authority then we are talking to the right person.

The people who do not qualify on these three aspects cannot take the decision independently. We can still talk to them because they may be the opinion makers but the person with AAA rating is the ultimate.

6. *What are the questions that we need to ask them?*

Ask more than you tell.

Many times, we assume that we know a lot about the prospect or the delegate. The answer in most cases is,'No'. It never hurts to ask for more information. It indicates to the other party that we are serious about our business and that we are interested in their choices and preferences. On the contrary, not asking questions might be perceived as audacity or ignorance.

Every prospect (be it a client or an investor) wants questions to be asked. They don't expect you to have answers to all questions. In fact, they will respect the people who ask the right questions.

The right questions will yield more answers and give you further clues as to what the expectations could be. It also elevates the ownership/involvement levels in the prospect.

7. *What do we expect from them towards the end of the journey?*

This is the ultimate question. What do we want?

- *Cheque to be cut immediately*

- *Agreement to be signed*
- *Pledge for more support*
- *Applause*

5 CHAPTER

THE RECIPE FOR SUCCESS

> "Getting things done is important, but it is not as vital as deciding what needs to be done."
>
> *- Unknown*

In this chapter, we will identify and gather the various ingredients required for our presentation. As described in the previous chapter, the content selection varies based on the context. It should be fine-tuned based on the following factors:

- *Objective*
- *Stakes involved*
- *Audience profile*
- *Structure of the showcase*
- *Time allotted for the actual presentation*

Content finalization is an iterative process that involves the following steps:

1. *Selection*
    - 1.1 *Information*
    - 1.2 *Insights*

- 1.2.1 *Case studies*
- 1.2.2 *Industry trends*
- 1.2.3 *Specific research reports*

1.3 *Interesting elements (spice)*

- 1.3.1 *Pictures, Silhouettes, Glyphs*
- 1.3.2 *Quotes*
- 1.3.3 *Cartoons and Caricatures*

1.4 *Facts and figures*

2. *Processing*

- 2.1 *Filtering*
- 2.2 *Refinement*
- 2.3 *Enrichment*

In this chapter, we will focus on the selection aspect and we will cover the processing part in the subsequent chapters.

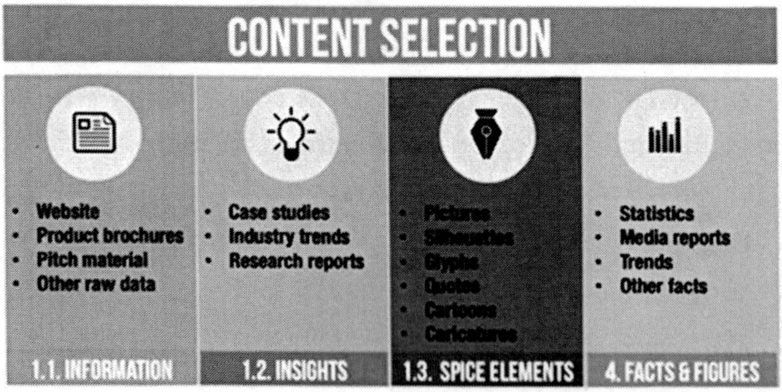

Figure 5.1

1. Content selection

Assuming that you are doing your first pitch with a prospect, ideally, the following features should be packed into your presentation:

- *A brief about the organization*

- *Key highlights of the product or service*
- *Unique Selling Propositions*
- *Benefits*
- *hat Is In It For Me for the prospect*
- *Case studies indicating problem statements of your clients and how the situation can be improved with your solution.*
- *Client references*
- *Why the prospect should choose your product/solution/service*

We will take this as a baseline and gather the content. At this stage we are not really worried about filtering the data or how to present it.

For now, we will just focus on information gathering.

Having identified the table of contents, we need to find various ingredients to enhance the offerings and spice them up further.

To start with, we will focus on the following areas:

1.1 *Information*

1.2 *Insights*

1.3 *Interesting elements (spice)*

1.4 *Facts and figures*

1.1. Information

It is usual for any organization to have reams of raw data. It could be in the form of brochures, product or service manuals, research papers, annual reports and so on. You may want to use as much of the raw material possible, in the presentation.

You may also be tempted to use the material from the marketing brochures, websites and old presentation archives.

Yes, we do need all this data. We must include the key messages from these content repositories. However, the problem comes when we try to copy and paste the contents as they are. I would suggest that you refrain from doing this.

This information should only complement the main pitch and cannot be standalone pitch material.

It is likely that the prospect would have already seen the content on your website before deciding to meet you.

Raw content, you will understand, is just plain vanilla data. It is either a chunk of text or mere numbers. To make the data meaningful, we need to convert this to information.

Pick the data from your website, media clippings, recent awards, key people profiles, product/service information.

As a person/group responsible for creating a strong presentation for the organization, you need to walk that extra mile to assess the current perception of the organization. You may be a direct stakeholder in the organization or you are representing the stakeholder (most likely, the CEO of your organization). Either way, you have to assume certain additional responsibilities on behalf of the CEO.

In any organization, the CEO has to wear two hats – one to assess the personality of the 'self' and the other to assess the personality of the organization that he is heading.

As the developer of the presentation, you need to gauge and assess these two parameters objectively.

Johari Window is an effective tool to explore the self-awareness of an individual. In case you are not aware of what this is, here is a quick explanation:

The window comprises of four quadrants. Two quadrants are known to the 'self' and others; the other two quadrants are unknown to the 'self' and others.

Johari Window

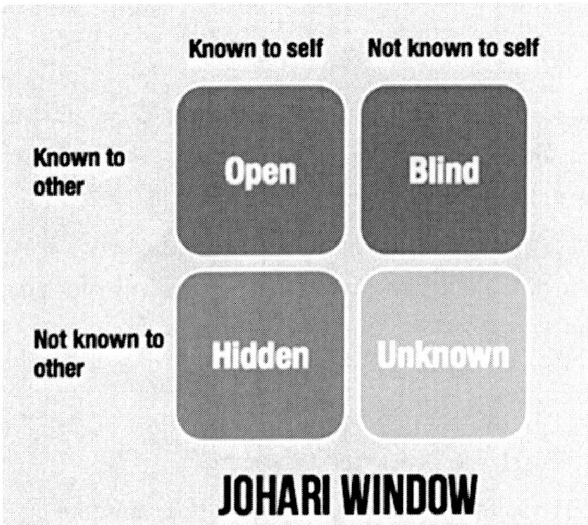

Figure 5.2

1. *Open Area: Known to everyone*
2. *Hidden Area: Known to 'self' but unknown to external people*
3. *Blind Spot: Unknown to 'self' but known to others*
4. *Unknown: No one knows about this*

Johari Window is primarily a tool to explore the self-awareness and personal development of an individual. To gauge the strengths and weaknesses of an organization, a SWOT analysis can be used.

However, this tool can give you a very good perspective into the organization, particularly when we want to present our strengths to prospects.

When it comes to managing perceptions and self-exploration, the organization we represent is similar to the personality of an individual.

Let's look at the **Johari window** *from an organizational perspective.*

Open area

This is public domain information. This is available on your website. Your employees, clients, prospects, competitors and virtually everyone in the industry knows this information.

Only the highlights of this information require to be put into the presentation. Too much of this is boring and dooms your prospects to boredom.

Hidden area

Only key stakeholders know this information.

We may need to selectively include this information, with utmost care and discretion. The following are some of the sources of this information.

1. *Financial information*
2. *Competitive intelligence reports*
3. *Organization's strategy*
4. *IP material*
5. *Confidential survey reports*
6. *USPs*
7. *Thought leadership*
8. *Future roadmap*
9. *The competitive edge that we are likely to gain in the near future with this information*
10. *Any other information that assures the prospect about the seriousness of the owners/key stakeholders in the business*

We need to present only the information that will portray the strengths of the organization.

Blind spot

This is the information, which has the potential to embarrass the presenter. If not handled properly, it could be the worst thing that could happen to any individual or organization.

This is also the most probable area from which most questions are likely to be asked. When the presenter is not fully prepared to handle the questions that are likely to be asked, he/she will look like a student facing an examiner asking an out of syllabus question.

Disgruntled employees and unhappy customers breed and nurture the blind spot.

This is found in the communication of disgruntled and disengaged employees. It is found in abundance in feedback forms and in complaint letters/emails, etc.from customers who are dissatisfied. This can also be found in the grapevine in the industry, lovingly fanned by competitors.

Search Twitter, Facebook and other social media sites. You will be surprised. Ask for the ageing reports of the complaints. You will be enlightened further.

The unknown

No one knows about this, so let's not worry about it at present.

1.2. Insights

Presenting insights is a sure shot way of earning the respect of your prospects. Insights not only enlighten the audience, but also give them the comfort that they are in the right hands.

We can draw insights from three sources:

1.2.1 Case studies

1.2.2 Industry trends

1.2.3 Research reports

1.2.1. Case studies

Case studies provide very good insights when presented to prospects, on how a particular product or solution can be implemented in a similar environment.

Business development teams often underplay this aspect. This could be because of lack of adequate information, lack of product/operational knowledge of the sales and marketing person.

A well-drafted case study should include the following:

1. *The client environment or problem area*
2. *The solution mix provided*
3. *The implementation model*
4. *The challenges faced and techniques used to overcome the challenges*
5. *Benefits realized by the client*
6. *Specific endorsements*

The above aspects effectively demonstrate various strengths of the organization like Solution Focus, Product/Service capability, team-work, execution abilities, etc.

This is a vital piece of the pitch material.

1.2.2. Industry trends

Industry trends could reflect changing technology adoption, consumer preference changes, research and development in the field.

Industry trends (local and global if available and relevant), when presented appropriately, can offer meaningful insights as well as effect the below:

1. *They educate the prospect*
2. *They tell the prospect that you are on top of things*

3. *Prospect gets assured that your business is being driven by a strategic intent behind*

1.2.3. Research Reports

Research reports if available can further strengthen your case and offer assurance to the prospect that they have approached the right organization.

1.3. Interesting elements (spice)

The 'spice' elements include the following:

1.3.1 Pictures, Silhouettes, Glyphs

1.3.2 Quotes

1.3.3 Cartoons and Caricatures

While there are no hard and fast rules for including these, we need to use the 'spice' elements in moderation. You can think of it as "adding salt to taste".

1.3.1 Pictures

One picture is worth a thousand words. You have heard this a thousand times and you just heard it once again!

The use of pictures has an incredible effect on the overall understanding of the presentation.

Collect the requisite pictures for every slide.

There are multiple sources for this. I find the following sites very useful:

1. *Shutterstock.com*
2. *Stockphotos for FREE.com*

These sites offer good images and abstract concepts. Just browsing through these images can trigger your creativity.

These are commercial sites and work based on subscription or on demand purchase. In case you are running on tight budgets or do not wish to spend on the images/pictures, you can evaluate the following open source repositories:

- *Wikimedia Creative Commons*
- *Flickr Creative Commons*
- *Stockvault.net*
- *freerangestock.com*
- *openphoto.net*

Some of the above sites directly offer downloads, while some of them ask you to login for a free registration. So, choose what suits you.

1.3.2 Quotes

The use of popular quotes can subtly open our communication channels and set the context in a succinct fashion. Again, there are free and paid sites for these.

1.3.3 Cartoons and caricatures

Cartoons can bring in the required humor and hook the audience further. This is however, a double-edged sword and must be used with thorough consideration of various parameters such as:

- *Speaker profile*
- *Delegate profile*
- *Context*
- *Overall relationship/bonding with the prospect*

- *Cultural aspects*
- *Other subtle details*

The best place to use this element is before a section/topic opening page or on the summary slide of a section/topic.

An appropriate cartoon at an appropriate time can do wonders and vice versa. However, use it with caution.

Note: For all these above options, you need to be acutely aware of the copyright/attribution related obligations. Over use of the above without proper copyright and attribution related obligations will not only project a very bad image of the organization, but in some cases, also invite legal troubles.

1.4. Facts and Figures

The data that we collect should be accurate. All claims we make around this should be verifiable and should demonstrate reasonable evidence.

As the famous quote from Edwards Deming says, "In God we trust; all others must bring data", we need to qualify the statements and claims with the relevant data.

We need to gather data like usage, performance trends, etc. In the next chapter, we will see various ways of presenting it.

6 CHAPTER

POSITIVE IMPACT

"The mind is the root from which all things grow if you can understand the mind, everything else is included."

– Swami Vivekananda

In the previous chapter, we have looked at various options and sources of gathering content. In this chapter, we will process the content and organize it into multiple slides.

Before we process the content, we will look at how our brains process the information before it is consumed. Needless to mention, we need to synchronize both, to avoid putting a square peg in a round hole.

How do our brains process information?

The so-called advanced technology that we use today has taken a heavy toll on our mental faculties, particularly on our attention spans. The higher the position someone holds in the organization, the less will be the attention span. This is irrespective of age. Without getting into the deep technicalities, let's discuss how our brains receive information.

> *During a party, one man asks another, "Do you eat like a human being or an animal?"*
>
> *Feeling embarrassed, the second man replied, "Of course, I eat like a human. What's the matter?"*
>
> *The first man smiles and says, "Oh. Then you eat more than your body needs."*
>
> *The reverse is also true for our brain.*
>
> **The brain is always on diet mode.**

Figure 6.1

Incoming traffic control and immigration checks

By default, our brains are very choosy in receiving and accepting information. They accept incoming messages only from trusted sources.

You can think of it as similar to the processing that takes place at an Immigration Check office.

The immigration check office tells us that there are two channels:

- *Red*
- *Green*

Any suspicious/prohibited materials need to be declared upfront and must pass through the Red channel.

If you have nothing to declare, you can go through the Green channel. The Green channel is quicker but if the EC officer finds anything that should have been declared, the passenger gets into a problem.

Our brains also have mini-immigration check offices inside. They process most of the information through these two channels.

Red channel

An average professional goes through over 100 direct and indirect marketing 'traps' in a day. Let's look at some of them:

1. *Offline advertisements on TV, radio, newspapers, magazines, boardings/billboards*
2. *Online advertisements: Cookie-powered web ads*
3. *Email marketing messages*
4. *Unsolicited tele-marketing calls (despite being on DND)*
5. *Location-based text messages*
6. *Social media updates*
7. *Other unsolicited sources*

In addition to the above, any other information received from a non-trust worthy source or from a person who is not very credible, is put through this scanner.

The prospect's mind is obviously choked, cluttered and inundated with these messages.

Material sent through this channel is always scanned for logic and reasoning adequacy.

Green channel

1. *Instructions coming from superiors (yes, this is a forced green channel entry. Spouse and mother-in-law included.)*
2. *Information from colleagues*
3. *other messages from trustworthy sources*
4. *Information perceived as trustworthy (when accompanied by relevant data points and evidences.)*
5. *This channel also gives room for a bit of emotional connect*

This channel is inundated with direct messages and instructions. While this channel appears to be an express path, this is also choked with more items that require action.

We need to adopt the most direct and unobtrusive methods to get our point across.

i-Channel

This is a hidden channel and not accessible to everyone. It only opens up to people who craft their messages carefully and follow all rules of the channel. Once the message enters this channel, it will override the decisions of other channels. The decision-making process is much faster and longer lasting.

This is called the i-Channel. This channel responds well to entertainment and emotions.

Children always communicate with parents through this channel. Needless to say, their success rate is above 100% in most cases.

This channel also accepts entertainment material. TV and cinema use this channel effectively.

Let's say that you have one hour of leisure time. You switch on the TV and find that the government channel is airing a very important program, which could be useful at your workplace. The program is for 20 minutes. Similarly, another channel is telecasting a blockbuster thriller movie featuring your favorite hero and heroine. This one is for three hours (two hours of movie and one hour of commercial breaks). Which one do you end up watching? Our leisure time is extended quietly.

That's the i-Channel. This channel is the most useful channel for airing presentations. Manage to get an entry through this channel and I am sure that your presentation will be a super success.

To do this, we need to mold our content and orient our messages to suit this channel. To do this effectively as well, we need to remove unwanted and redundant content from our repository of information. We will do all these in a short while from now.

At this stage you may think, "Why do we need to spend so much time on the content? Why can't we jump to PowerPoint and start creating our slides and add the information as required?"

We need to focus on the design aspects without losing sight of our content. Design should be based on engineering and vice versa.

There is a popular belief that our slides should contain a balance of color, images, etc. Having the right balance is very essential. However, content also needs to be included in the balance.

Figure 6.2

In figure 6.2, the images and colors look balanced. However, does the message sync with the background? What about the mental balance of the person reading the message?

Figure 6.3

In Figure 6.3, the message has dump yard as its background picture. But the message is a positive one.

While visuals and creativity are important for a presentation, syncing it with strong content should be your focus.

Creating well-rounded pegs

Before we begin, let's look at the famous Triple Filter Test of communication. This is an old and evergreen test prescribed by the great philosopher Socrates.

Triple Filter Test

One day an acquaintance met Socrates and said, "Do you know what I just heard about your friend?"

"Hold on a minute," Socrates replied. "Before you talk to me about my friend, it might be good idea to take a moment and filter what you are going to say. That's why I call it the triple filter test. The first filter is Truth. Have you made absolutely sure that what you are about to tell me is true?"

"Well, no," the man said, "actually I just heard about it and..."

"All right," said Socrates. "So you don't really know if it's true or not. Now, let's try the second filter, the filter of Goodness. Is what you are about to tell me about my friend something good?"

"Umm, no, on the contrary..."

"So," Socrates continued, "you want to tell me something bad about my friend, but you are not certain that it's true. You may still pass the test though, because there's one filter left—the filter of Usefulness. Is what you want to tell me about my friend going to be useful to me?"

"No, not really."

"Well," concluded Socrates, "if what you want to tell me is neither true, nor good, nor even useful, why tell it to me at all?"

The triple filter test is applicable while dealing with any type of communication. We need to find a similar filter for presentations!

SIMPLE framework: The six stage content refinement process

The temptation to pack in as much information as possible can undermine a person who is creating a presentation.

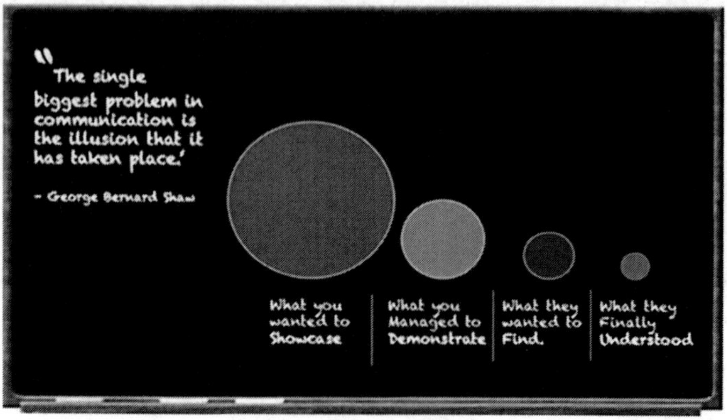

Figure 6.4

You think PowerPoint. The audience thinks Pressure Point. The SIMPLE filter is what converts it from Pressure Point to Pleasure Point.

We need to make sure that our slideshow does not end up as a horror show.

To transform our slideshow into a magic show, we have a special six-stage filter called SIMPLE.

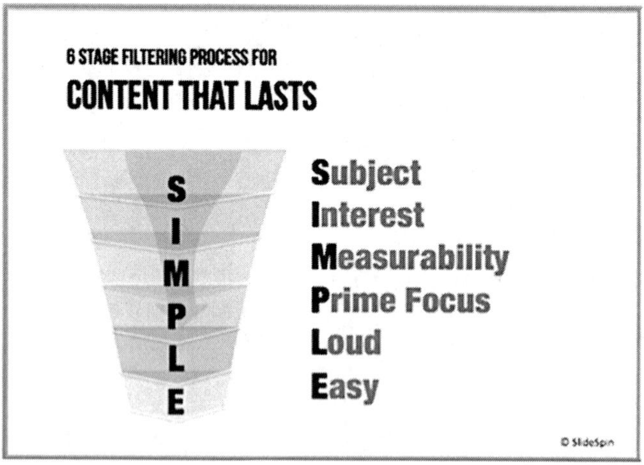

Figure 6.5

- *Relevant to the current* **Subject or Solution**
- *Covers listeners'* **Interest** *and context*
- *Contains only* **Measurable** *statements and claims*
- *Has a* **Prime Mover Point**
- *All messages expressed* **Loud** *and* **Clear**
- *Is* **Easy** *on the eye and the mind*

To understand the concept better, let's look at the figure 6.6.

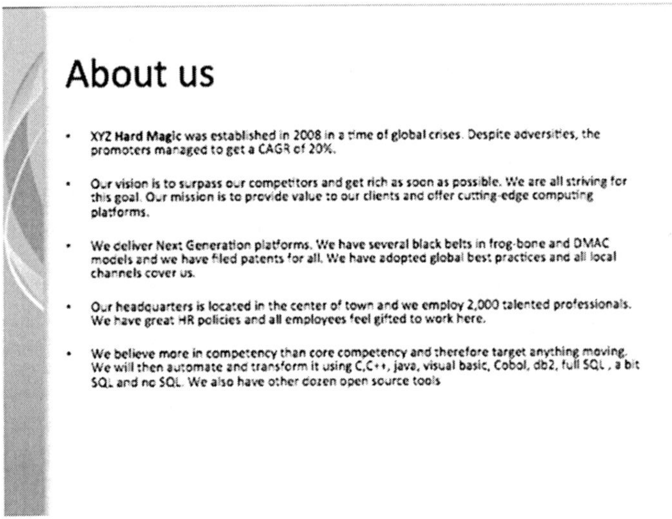

Figure 6.6

The 'About us' slide in figure 6.6 adopts the well-known essay style of presentation.

It uses yet another standard Power Point template, which though neat and adequate, is just that – adequate and boring.

Since the font size has been chosen in order to fit all the material in one slide, the content is not readable. Given below is the content of the slide:

> *XYZ* **Hard Magi**c *was established in 2008 in a time of global crises. Despite adversities, the promoters managed to get a CAGR of 20%.*
>
> *Our vision is to surpass our competitors and get rich as soon as possible. We are all striving for this goal. Our mission is to provide value to our clients and offer cutting-edge computing platforms.*
>
> *We deliver Next Generation platforms. We have several black belts in frog-bone and DMAC models and we have filed patents for all. We have adopted global best practices and all local channels cover us.*
>
> *Our headquarters is located in the center of town and we employ 2,000 talented professionals. We have great HR policies and all employees feel gifted to work here.*
>
> *We believe more in competency than core competency and therefore target anything moving. We will then automate and transform it using C, C++, java, visual basic, Cobol, db2, full SQL, a bit SQL and no SQL. We also have other dozen open source tools.*

It starts with the history of the company and goes on to explain the vision and mission. It also throws up jargons and over-used phrases like value-addition, global, next generation, transformation, etc. Finally it boasts about HR policies.

What do we call this? **Slide Salad!**

Our objective is to transform the slide into something that is shown in Figure: 6.7 and eventually transform it into what is shown in Figure: 6.8.

About us

- 100 clients
- 10 locations
- 10 years in the business
- More than 30 products in use
- Over 100 solutions deployed
- Over 20 similar solutions implemented
- 50% repeat customers
- 30% YoY growth

Figure 6.7

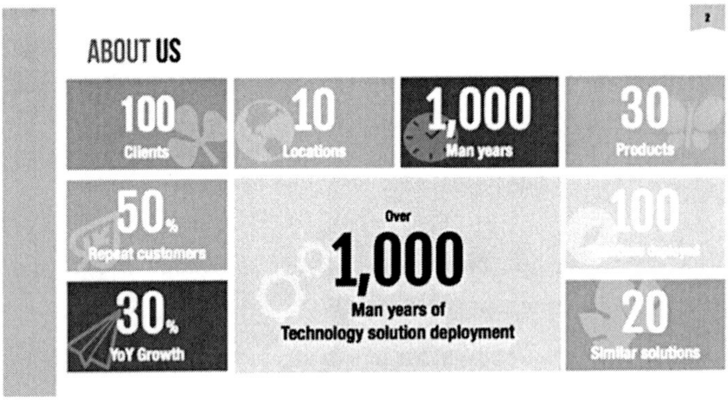

Figure 6.8

1. Subject orientation

What is 'subject'? It is your idea or concept that you want to sell to your colleagues or teammates. It could also be a solution, product or service that you are marketing for your customers and prospects.

Draw a boundary line and make sure that the content stays within that boundary.

Each slide should necessarily contain references to the solution that the prospect is looking for. While it is extremely tempting to showcase everything that we have, the prospect may not be interested in looking at all of them at once. By packing more, we are only diluting the main message.

Every slide should directly or indirectly strengthen the case in hand – i.e. the solution we are providing or the problem that we are solving. If the items we present do not refer to this central theme, then they are redundant.

If the client finds your statements to be sensible, he or she will instantly acknowledge them, unless someone wants to purposefully control the appreciation. This could be through body language or through verbal statements. The client may then begin a discussion, after this.

2. Interest

Will a client give you business because he/she wants to see your balance sheet getting stronger?

Similarly,will your boss listen to you just because he is committed to doubling your salary this year?

No. People listen when it is relevant or is of interest to them. Everyone wants to find the answer to his or her prime question: What Is In It For Me? Only WIIFM. Nothing else.

3. Measurable

Our data, information, claims, promises, statements and anything that we state should be measurable. If we have a point or a claim that is not measurable, we cannot compare it with anything, there is no improvement for it; there is no way to verify it.

If it is abstract, it is misleading. Drop it.

Misleading information also includes the following:

1. *Any statement or a claim that cannot be verified*
2. *Inconsistent and contradictory data points*
3. *Incorrect data/false statements that challenge publicly available data*
4. *Any piece of information that dilutes the main focus or takes audience away from the prime mover item*
5. *Drop any information that is misleading.*

4. Prime Mover

Prime Mover is something that powers the rest of the parts. The Prime Mover ignites and set things in motion. Identify one such bullet item which is the most important one, and that provides meaning and context to the rest of the points.

Assume that you are organizing a dance show on a large stage/ podium with thousands of people in front of it. How many lead performers do you have on the stage? One? Two? More? Obviously one or at best two. If we have more, they are not called lead performers.

Same rule is applicable for Slide Shows. Think of each slide as a large stage/podium. Having more than 6 bullets results in a SlideMob situation. You need to have one prime mover item that clearly conveys the main message of the slide.

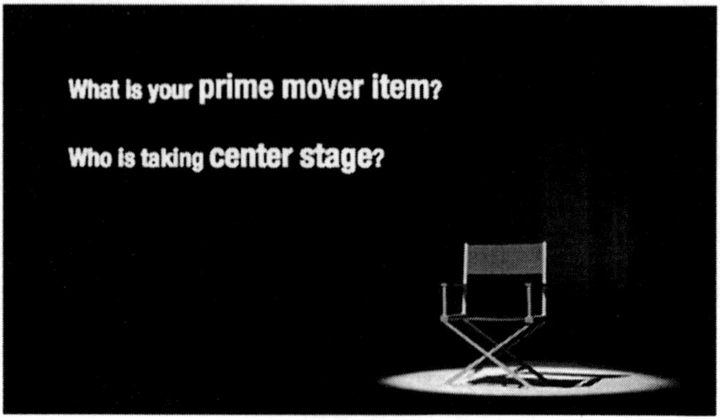

Figure 6.9

The next question is: What is the Prime Mover bullet point on the slide? Which item would you put center stage? Where should the focus light be pointed?

5. Loudness

Points should be direct and convey the meaning loud and clear. Indirect messages will confuse, distract and become boring.

State the benefits, possible issues and expectations upfront without beating around the bush. Everyone appreciates a can did approach.

6. Ease

The Presenter and Audience are at the core here. They should be at ease with the slides. The presenter should be able to explain them easily and the audience should not find them difficult to understand.

Ease can be enhanced or compromised by the following:

1. *Text*
2. *Text Size*

3. Numbers
4. Charts
5. Colors
6. Fonts
7. Layout & Formatting

We will look at colors, fonts and layout in the next section. We will now discuss text, text size, numbers and charts. If these are long and cluttered, the overall message loses clarity and crispness. Each of these three elements needs to be tuned, toned and seasoned.

The following are the broad guidelines:

6.1 Text

This is an area where we need to spend a lot of time, and carryout multiple iterations to achieve succinctness.

Each bullet point in the slide should be revised multiple times until we arrive at a crisp message within 6 to 8 words.

To the extent possible, eliminate the following:

- Unwanted English: Excessive use of adjectives, repetitive words and expressions
- Archaic, poetic and textbook expressions
- Redundant phrases like 'at the end of the day', 'needless to say', 'it is pertinent to mention', 'we made an analysis of', 'we are in agreement with', etc.
- Technical jargons
- Over-used business vocabulary like 'value-addition', 'game changing', and 'cutting edge'
- Passive voice

To pack further power into bullet points, check the following sources for to see if the messages are crisp and clear:

1. *Vision and Mission Statements*
2. *Famous Tweets*
3. *Famous Quotes*
4. *Concise expressions*
5. *Punch lines and Taglines*
6. *High concept and elevator pitches*

While the items 1, 2 and 3 are self-explanatory, we will spend a minute on#4,#5, and #6:

6.1.4. Concise expressions

How do you define a straight line? The mathematical explanation states, "It is the shortest possible distance between two points."

Similarly concise expressions are a set of words that convey the whole meaning of the message in the least number of words.

Eg: Work Works.

Another example of such a crisp expression is by Mr.Calvin Coolidge.

The following is an excerpt from the David Pietrusza's book Silent Cal's Almanac: The Homespun Wit and Wisdom of Vermont's Calvin Coolidge

> *American President Calvin Coolidge had a reputation in private of being a man of few words and was nicknamed "Silent Cal". A possibly apocryphal story has it that a matron seated next to him at a dinner said to him, "I made a bet today that I could get more than two words out of you." His reply: "You lose."*

6.1.5 Punch lines and taglines

Punch lines and taglines will amplify the meaning of the slide. You don't need to add taglines for every slide. Ideally, you can use one for the opening slide, the product benefits slide and the 'Why us?'slide.

Observe popular taglines. Try and see if you can express your feelings and emotions in the right context. Don't use jargon, exaggeration or lengthy phrases. Mix subtle humor if possible.

Eg: For the product benefit slide you can say: "Small Price. Large Gains."

Alternatively you can try rhyming dictionaries online. Eg: "Easy as a toy, brings you joy" or "Feels like a toy while you deploy".

6.1.6 High Concept

Movies use a special pitch called High Concept Pitch. This is a very effective way of explaining the crux in the simplest manner. Observe the trailers of popular films. Read the introduction paragraphs behind DVD/Blu-ray discs. They all convey the entire story in a few lines. They induce interest and evoke curiosity.

To sum up, you should be able to send each slide as an SMS or a tweet. If it is longer than that, you have some pending work on the slide!

6.2 Text Size

Text size plays a major role in the overall communication of the presentation.

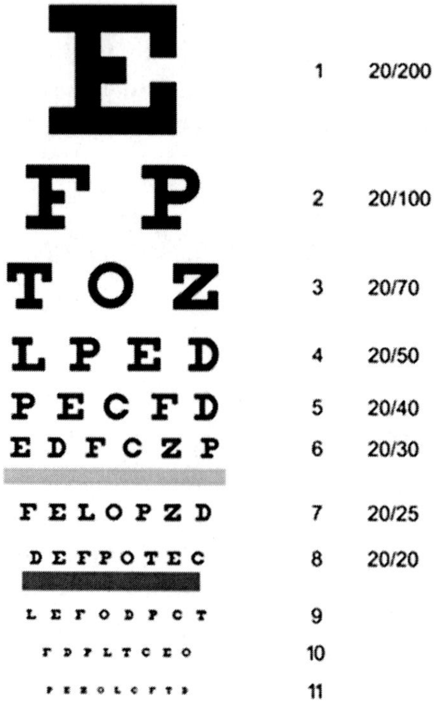

Figure 6.10

If you have ever visited an eye doctor, you would have seen the chart shown in Figure 6.10. Eye doctors make us sit 20 feet away from this board and ask us to read the letters on it. 99% people comfortably read the first four rows of letters. In most countries, a driving license is given to those with minimum 20/40 eyesight with or without eye-wear. So, it is safe to assume that the same standards apply for our presentations too.

Since our objective is not to test either eyesight or patience, we will try to match the font size of the first four rows.

Assuming the average conference room length to be less than 20 feet and assuming that we use projectors, the smallest font size on the slide should be 18 points or more.

6.3 Numbers

Every statement or claim we make should be verifiable and must be qualified with the relevant data points.

As the famous quote by Edward Deming states, "We believe in god, others must bring data."

There are many memory techniques to present data by chunking, logically separating it to make it simpler to comprehend, etc.

However, the intent of the presentation is to explain the meaning or the impact of the numbers that we present. We need not go overboard in making the prospects remember and learn them by heart. Therefore, presenting numbers beyond three or four digits could lead to different issues.

You need to make the numbers readable, comprehendible and relatable.

The best way to present the numbers is to round them to the closest high measure and format them with units of measure and commas.

Let's assume that you need to explain the weight of an elephant to a 2nd grade student. Suppose you say, "It weighs approximately 300000000 milligrams."

How will the child relate to this?

You could probably say, "It weighs more than all your classmates put together." The child will be able to appreciate a conversion factor that he is familiar with or at least a concept that he can relate to. Elders are no exception to this.

Eg: If you are presenting Revenue or Expenditure figures, round them to the nearest '000.

It is simpler to mention $ 100,000 or Mil $100

To bring more perspective, add ↓↑to indicate the change in values compared to the previous reporting period.

6.4 Charts

Charts offer an excellent opportunity to bring perspective to numbers.

Unfortunately, this is an area where a large number of disasters happen. Therefore, we need to think of really 'out-of-the-box' to ensure that we do a good job or showcasing this.

We have probably learnt our first lessons in pre-school with pictures and graphs. We have forgotten this in our growing years. We should recall our childhood experiences and learn to create impressive pictographs.

Passing the SIMPLE test of simplicity

Let us now look at a case study to try out the SIMPLE test. I have considered a B2B scenario again because this is the most complex situation, with relatively high stakes involved. The test however, is universally applicable.

In the previous chapter, we have listed out the agenda items. Those are as follows:

1. *A brief about the organization*
2. *Key benefits of the product or service*
3. *Unique Selling Propositions*
4. *Case studies indicating the problem statements of your clients and how the situation improved with your solution*
5. *Rollout or Implementation plan*

6. *Summary: Why the prospect should choose your product/ solution/service*

We will now build each of these slides with the information that we have gathered so far.

Slide # 1 | A brief about the organization

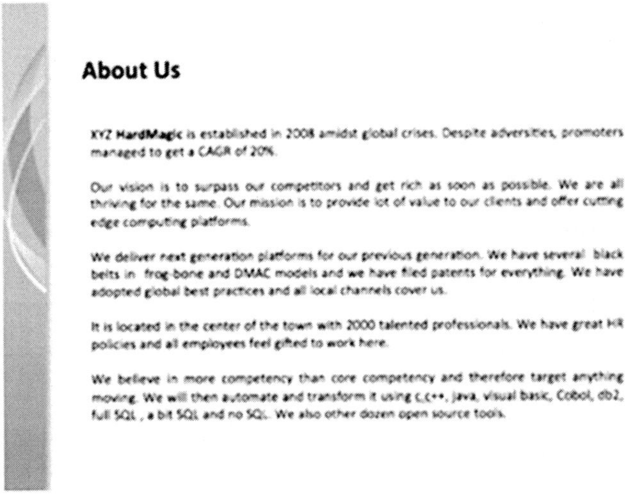

Figure 6.11

Back to the main context:

1. *Remember, you are familiarizing your organization to a hot prospect*
2. *The person with AAA rating will be in the room*
3. *All brains are on 'diet' mode*
4. *None of the delegates have any plans of joining our organization. So, let's drop all material that look like they are meant for company induction*
5. *They are not going to write an exam on your organization either. So, drop all intricate history.*

Pick up the following:

- *# Clients*
- *# Locations*
- *# Years in the business*
- *# Products in use/Solutions deployed*
- *# Similar solutions implemented*
- *# Repeat customers*
- *# YoY growth*

It is not possible for a start-up company to demonstrate the above items. In that case, the overview can be presented like in a CV.

- *# People*
- *# Key Strengths (Skills, Achievements, Awards and Accolades)*
- *# Beliefs*
- *# Objective of starting the organization*
- *# Vision, Mission and Values*

Slide 1 | SIMPLE Test

S	*Within the subject boundary*
	Contains only the relevant facts and statistics that strengthen the solution.
I	*Within the interest. Dropped all un-wanted content used in Induction, History, etc.,*
M	*Only measurable content and data is included. All misleading and conflicting information is dropped.*
P	*Has a Prime Mover item.*
L	*No prose and essay. Contains only concise/brief expressions. Message is loud and clear.*
E	*Contents are easy to read and understand*

Simple expressions. No complex data points for prospects to remember.

Slide # 2 | Key benefits of the product or service

Many a time, even good sales people get confused between a feature and benefit.

Explaining the feature is only a verbose way of confusing the prospect and driving him or her away.

Prospects come to you in search of a solution to their problem/s.

Your organization has developed a service or a product to address a specific client problem. Sometimes, clients and prospects may not be aware of their problem. They may also be ignorant of a new solution that can make their life simpler.

Customers choose products with certain expectations. We need to demonstrate the What Is In It For Me message clearly. This can happen only while illustrating the benefits. The benefits include one or more of the following:

- ☑ *Cost cutting*
- ☑ *No capital expenses or cost variabilization*
- ☑ *Productivity improvement*
- ☑ *Faster to time to market*
- ☑ *Consistent results/output*
- ☑ *Convenience*
- ☑ *Scalability*
- ☑ *Overall cost savings*

The above factors need to be demonstrated with measurable numbers. All of these ultimately roll up to overall cost savings. So, it should be the key focus element.

Checklist compliance: SIMPLE test

S	*Within the subject boundary*
	Contains only the relevant facts and stats
I	*Does not contain product features*
M	*Has only measurable information*
P	*Identified the Prime Mover.*
L	*No prose and essays. Contains only numbers.*
E	*No English. No roundabout expressions. Simple and verifiable data points. Easy to understand and explain.*

Slide # 3 | Unique Selling Propositions

As a next logical step, after understanding the benefits, clients will get into comparison mode.

You need to clarify two items immediately:

1. *What sets you apart from the closest competitor?*
2. *What do prospects lose if they don't choose you? In statistical quality control, there are two types of errors defined. The error in choosing a wrong product and the error in rejecting a right product. You need to subtly warn them of this double-trouble situation that they are likely to get into.*

Unique Selling Propositions include the following:

- *Proprietary/patented techniques*
- *Service reach*
- *24/7 Support*
- *Free upgrades*
- *Discounted service fees*
- *Multiple delivery channels*
- *Availability of SMEs*

However, these are very generic. You should be able to identify very specific items once you speak to your product design team. Existing customers who are very loyal your organization could give you plenty of insights into this. Don't assume that you know everything about your organization. On any day, for any enterprise, no employee can match the collective knowledge of a customer about the product/service.

You need to similarly list out the good things that a client is likely to miss if they don't consider your solution.

Checklist Compliance: SIMPLE test

S	Within the subject boundary.
I	Does not contain product features.
M	Information given is completely measurable and does not contain any misleading facts or statements.
P	Identified the Prime Mover.
L	No prose and essays. Contains only numbers.
E	Direct bullets. Easy to understand.

Slide 4: Case studies

This is story time. This is probably the best ever time to boast, brag and showcase what you have achieved.

Articulation of a case study can potentially make the presentation memorable and successful.

We are packing important material for the I-Channel. If this channel opens up, our job is done.

I personally begin to present by narrating the story of a successful case study. The story can captivate the audience and give us the hook to hold them till the end of the presentation. By the time we finish the case study, they are fully aware of the benefits of the solution and what they would lose in case they reject it. Stories should contain subtle references to clients as well as the USPs.

The presentation can then be used to recap and strengthen the message. Finally, we can give an overview about the organization and thank them for listening.

In general, most presenters start by thanking the audience and explaining how grateful they are to the whole world for the opportunity. They should be awarded for bringing in the boredom effortlessly, at the beginning itself. If the opening is not strong, then the rest of the presentation will only be as effective. You could include the following items in the case study:

1. *Client situation: One or two lines*
2. *Solution designed: One or two lines*
3. *Timeframe*
4. *Total team*
5. *Deal size*
6. *Outcomes/benefits to clients: Quantifiable measures*

Checklist compliance: SIMPLE test

S	*Within the subject boundary. Contains only the relevant facts and stats.*
I	*Most relevant examples picked in the case study.*
M	*Information given is completely measurable and does not contain any misleading facts or statements.*
P	*Identified the Prime Mover.*
L	*No prose and essays. Contains only numbers.*
E	*All complexity of words, numbers mellowed down. It is simple to explain and understand.*

Slide 5: Rollout/Implementation plan

Help the clients visualize the journey. Through the presentation, you need to wear the hat of a 'friend' or a 'guide' rather than a 'seller hat'. You can close more deals by being a friend rather than being a mere seller.

It is therefore essential to help the client visualize the journey by explaining the various steps or milestones involved.

At this stage, this need not be a perfect project plan but should indicate crucial elements like timelines, specific requirements, outcomes and other interdependent items.

Slide 6: Summary

The summary slide is just the recap of all the Prime Mover items. To make it interesting, you can also include one-on-one comparison with the nearest competitor. This is also the time to exchange commitments.

CHAPTER 7

THE SPARK

> "When the flower blooms, the bees come uninvited."
> *- Ramakrishna Paramahamsa*

In the previous chapter, we have looked at the techniques to fine-tune the content. In this chapter, we will enhance the content and make it visually appealing.

It is time for us to open PowerPoint now. Notice that we have not looked at the PowerPoint till we made sure that we have a strong plan and content.

About us

- 100 clients
- 10 locations
- 10 years in the business
- More than 30 products in use
- Over 100 solutions deployed
- Over 20 similar solutions implemented
- 50% repeat customers
- 30% YoY growth

Figure 7.1

This time, there is no clutter and unwanted information. However, this is not good enough to present. Let us look at various ways of enhancing the slide.

Visual appeal is achieved by using and adjusting the following:

1. *Aspect Ratio*
2. *Display Resolution*
3. *Color*
4. *Font*
5. *Glyphs*
6. *Silhouettes*
7. *Pictures*
8. *Infographics*
9. *Geometric shapes*
10. *Audio*
11. *Video*

Aspect ratio

Aspect ratio refers to the ratio of the width of an image to the height of the image.

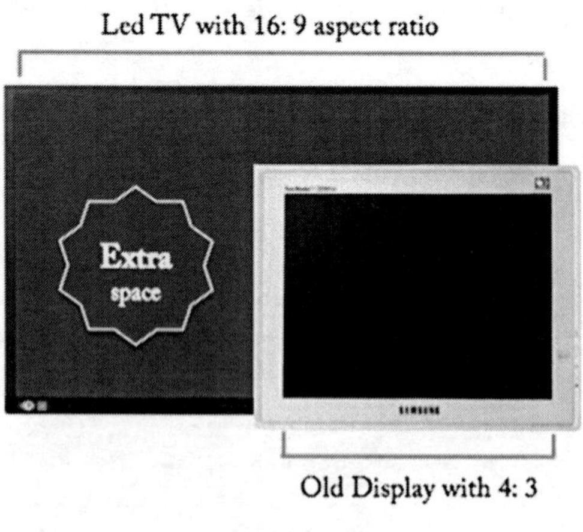

Figure 7.2

We discarded the old CRT monitors almost a decade ago, but we continue to use the 4:3 aspect ratio, perhaps in memory of the CRT!

4:3 The aspect ratio limits the size and the number of the enhancements that we can do to the slide. 16:9 in aspect ratio not only gives more room but fits in optimally in the recent monitors, TVS and other displays.

We are going to make use of this additional 'real estate' to pack in a few good features.

Display resolution

"Super AMOLED, Retina, Ultra HD, Quad HD, 4K..."

Have you heard the above buzz words in the recent past?

Now look at the image below:

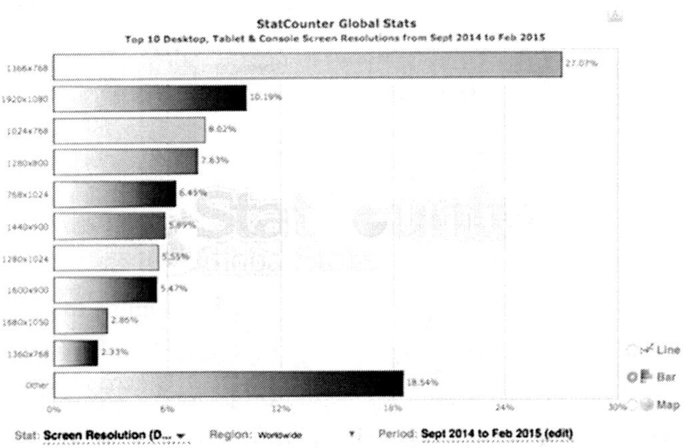

Figure 7.3

Source:http://gs.statcounter.com/#resolution-ww-monthly-201409-201502-bar

What do these statistics tell us? Simple.

1. *The war for the best display is getting hotter*

2. *We can expect to hear a few more buzz words*
3. *Display resolution and holes in our wallet are becoming larger and larger*

You will also notice that the standard and the most popular resolution is 1366 × 768

Colors

Fonts and colors are subjective. Handle them with care.

If you are working on your corporate presentation deck, you might want to align the colors with your logo and branding rules.

If you still feel that you can avoid the standard colors, consider the following:

PowerPoint gives you a good variety of universal color themes. We can safely use those because we can assume that considerable amount of research went into its design before the PowerPoint version was released.

If you look at Vibgyor, the first four colors are called cool colors and the last three are warm colors. Warm colors are aggressive and cool colors are calm and serene.

Fortunately, there are plenty of tools available online to guide us on this.

Many a time, we want to know what colors have been used in pictures, graphics or other images. There are tools to help you discover this. If you search Google, with keywords like "color picker", you will get many tools. Try two or three of these before making your choice.

Sometimes despite identifying the color we want to use, we may be indecisive about the color combination. You can try www.colorcombos.com. It gives basic template color combinations that can help you in most scenarios. You can also try http://colorschemedesigner.com. This site allows you to choose one base color and suggests color combinations for using this as a reference point. I suggest you choose pastel colors as the base. You will get good results. Similarly try http://www.colorhunter.com/. This site also gives color palettes with real life pictures as preview examples. If you are not satisfied, Google again with keywords "color combo".

Sometimes, we may want to insert a picture or photo and would want the rest of the slide to have a complementary color. http://www.pictaculous.com/ accepts image uploads and suggests color palettes.

I am not going into cookbook mode here, because these are self-explanatory tools.

Try these tools and use a balanced approach with not more than three colors per slide. Most importantly, maintain color consistency.

Fonts

To use fonts effectively, you need to understand the following:

1. *The primary intent of your the presentation: Print or screen show*
2. *Types of fonts by Typography: Serif and Sans Serif*
3. *Subject/genre of your presentation*
4. *Impact of fonts and font sizes.*

You need to be clear about the intent or the main use of our slides. Are they going to be printed? Or would you be using them as slideshow?

Based on the intent of your presentation, you can select images, fonts and other graphic elements.

There are specialized and separate fonts for on-screen display and print media.

Font types: You often hear words like Serif and Sans Serif. Here is a quick explanation of the concept:

Figure 7.4

Use Sans-Serif fonts if you are aiming for on–screen presentation. They are clear and readable at any size.

Use Serif fonts if your presentation is going to be printed out and given as handouts.

Don't use cursive, script and handwriting fonts. They are hard to read.

The following figure illustrates the possible fonts for various purposes.

Figure 7.5

Organizations spend millions on logo, branding, etc. They often ignore the power of a unique font. There are popular brands that have exploited the power of fonts and made them a part of their branding. Coco Cola, Ferrari, Puma, Yahoo, Ford, Studds, etc. are some of the best examples.

Like colors, fonts are also very subjective and the preferences change from person to person. Font types follow fashion trends like any other design product. Since the majority of Mankind uses either an MS or Apple PC/Laptop, it is best to stick to the fonts used by them. The current trend is the use of Lucida Grande and Segoe UI for Apple and MS versions of Operating Systems respectively.

Assuming that the conference room length is less than 20 feet and you are using a projector, the smallest font size should not be below 18 point.

We will apply the lessons learned so far:

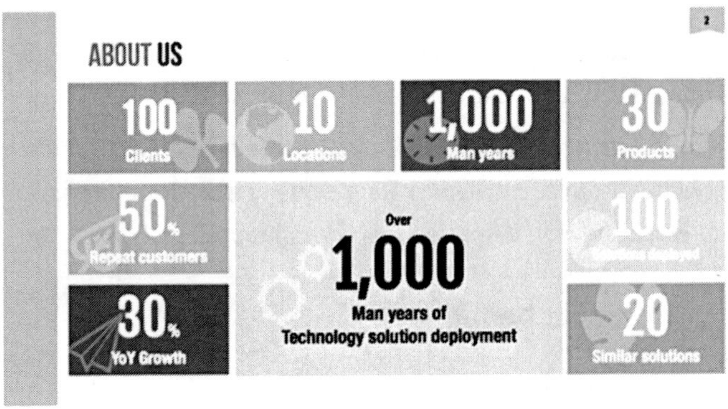

Figure 7.6

We have done the following changes:

- *Changed the slide layout to 16:9.*
- *Used bold and tall fonts for the heading.*
- *Used strong 'Sans' type fonts for the content*

- *Highlighted numbers*
- *Used metro style icons*
- *Identified the Prime Mover item and put this in the centre*

The current trend is also flat themes. If you have observed the latest operating systems like Windows 8, Mac Yosemite or IOS (iPhone, iPAD), etc., you will notice the difference. No icon, picture or shape comes with 3D effects or shadows.

Since this trend has come in recently, we will be safe in using it for another couple of years. In my opinion, using excessive shadows, colors, etc. in a presentation will certainly make it look old-fashioned. Eg: How would you perceive someone who greets you wearing a bell-bottomed trouser and a loose and flowery shirt? Shadows and other embellishments are just that – dated.

Glyph

Glyphs are special type of lightweight icons embedded in fonts. Wingdings and Webdings are the popular examples.

There is a general tendency to use the standard bullets for the text used. Most often, each bullet item conveys a separate message. We can break the monotony by using the appropriate Glyph.

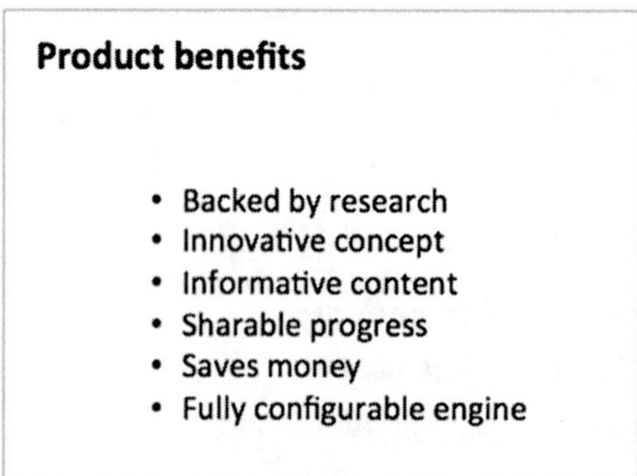

Figure 7.7

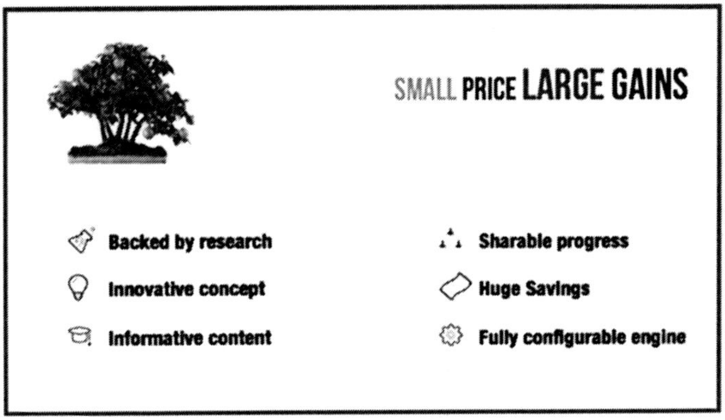

Figure 7.8

Look at the figures 7.7 and 7.8. The content is same in both the slides. However, we have enhanced the second slide with fonts, colors, images and glyphs.

When we present the information with pictures and images, people look at those first and understand the message. When they read the text, the message is reinforced. Overall, comprehension becomes a simple affair.

Glyphs are lightweight, i.e. they consume less space. If you use images as an alternative to Glyphs, your file size will become bigger. Because of their small sizes, Glyphs can be used for websites to. They are sharp in even small dimensions.

There are various sources for Glyphs. In recent times, there is an evolution of web-based fonts and one such popular font is called 'Font Awesome'.

http://fontawesome.io/

There are 470 icons in this font and the beauty is that it is open source and license-free.

Silhouette

A silhouette is an outlined and darker version of any shape.

There are occasions when you don't want to show the actual picture of someone in the slide. This could be because of reasons of anonymity or because the picture might take the focus away from the actual subject/message.

Figure 7.9

In such situations, using a silhouette is the best option. We will also be able to create silhouettes from photos very easily. We will cover more of this subject in the next section.

PowerPoint RaCreD

The world has moved from character-based systems to graphics-based systems during the late 80s and the early 90s. Soon after the GUI-based operating systems were released, Microsoft announced Visual Basic for developing commercial/business applications on Windows. VB is a Rapid Development Tool. That means, what requires 100 lines of coding in traditional programming languages, could be accomplished in VB with less than 10 lines of code and a few mouse clicks.

Obviously, the demand for VB programmers grew leaps and bounds. Although this phenomena has obviously annoyed core C/C++ programmers, the evolution continued. But the fact is that VB never competed with C++ or Java. It only made the life of the entry level programmer better. The rest is history.

Similarly, PowerPoint offers us Rapid Creative Development (RaCreD) facilities, which are easy for entry-level designers and novice users. What is a complex sequence of steps in tools like Photoshop can be done in a few clicks in PowerPoint.

PowerPoint does have limitations but a regular user may not encounter this at all – it would take a lifetime for an entry level or middle level designer to hit any roadblock or limitations in this software.

The two important features for Rapid Creative Design are Pictures and Shapes. PowerPoint conceals many complexities from us and presents easy-to-use and intuitive controls for creative designing. So, you can focus on what you need to create rather than how you can create it. Isn't it convenient?

An innovative brain breaks the complexity and the monotony. We will test our innovation skills with these two features.

Pictures

Use of pictures really boosts the impact of the overall message. Pictures make slides more presentable and meaningful. There is a general misconception that PowerPoint is very primitive in handling pictures. This general belief makes us believe that we need special skills to handle images and that one needs to know how to use products like Photoshop or something more complex.

But the good news is that PowerPoint is really versatile in handling images and a novice user can really do a professional job.

The real beauty of this feature is that it takes less than 30 minutes to learn it.

Let us now look at the different scenarios for picture usage/ manipulation and try to understand how to achieve the desired results in less than 10 clicks for each.

You can download a bonus chapter on image tools from http:// slidespinners.com. It contains step-by-step instructions for the various techniques explained in the book.

Photo to silhouette

Let's assume that you want to convey a message about freedom, simplicity or a similar concept. You will probably search for related images but will soon realize that the images available online are either too expensive or are unsuitable.

The best way then, is to take a photograph of the concept yourself and convert it into a silhouette.

Figure: 7.11 (Image Courtesy: StockphotosforFREE.com)

Since you are going to use a silhouette only, you don't need to be concerned about complex photography skills.

The following are the quicksteps to achieve this:

1. *Insert the picture for which you need the silhouette*
2. *Copy the image and paste it next to the original image*
3. *Select the new image*
4. *Right click on the image and select Format Picture*
5. *Select Adjust Picture*
6. *Decrease the brightness till the image becomes completely dark*
7. *To fine-tune the image further, adjust the contrast and sharpness as required*

Note: You don't need to be concerned about the quality of your camera or your photography skills. All you need to know are a few photo manipulation and enhancement skills. The primary intent of taking a photo in this instance is to enhance the message in your presentation and not to win a photography contest. So, the camera on your smart phone will suffice. You can rise to the occasion by just aiming and shooting.

Color blending with image

Let's say that you have an image and you want to enhance it by adding a caption or a quote. You also want to make sure that the caption is part of the image and want to ensure that the caption blends with the image seamlessly.

Figure:7.12

You can do this by setting the picture style to 'soft edge rectangle' and by changing the color of the background shape to blue, with the color picker tool. This one can also be achieved in less than five clicks.

Figure 7.13: (Image Courtesy: StockphotosforFREE.com)

Once you have the image without the background, you can choose where to place the subject. It can be a beach, a bus stop, a mountain landscape and so on.

3D effect

Figure: 7.14

You can also create 3D effects as shown above. It is a struggle to achieve a similar effect in Photoshop. Take a look at a video that will demonstrate this, by typing, "3d effect in Photoshop" in YouTube. This feature is ridiculously simple in PowerPoint. We can create this effect in less than five clicks as well.

Note: The objective here is not to put down other creative tools. The author is only trying to highlight the useful features of PowerPoint.

Background blur

Background blur is used in two contexts.

1. When you want to create a slide background from an image
2. When you want to highlight a portion of the image to draw attention

The process in both cases is similar. PowerPoint offers great facilities to manipulate images under the 'Artistic effects' menu item. For now, we will only cover the blur option.

Let's look at the images in figure 7.15.

Original image Blurred image

Figure: 7.15

The blurred image can be used as a slide background. Try the following steps:

1. *Copy and paste the original image*
2. *Right click on the copied image*
3. *Select format picture*
4. *Select 'blur' option from the artistic filters option*
5. *Adjust the radius till you get the desired result*

Sometimes, when we take a photo, we only want to show portions of it or focus on select objects.

Look at the pictures in figure 7.16

Original image Focus image

Figure: 7.16 (Image Courtesy: StockphotosforFREE.com)

We have picked up only one dancer from the four in this picture and highlighted her.

Try the following steps:

1. *Copy and paste the original image*
2. *Right click on the copied image*
3. *Select format picture*
4. *Select 'blur' option from the artistic filters option*

Object focus

There are occasions when you want to focus only on a particular portion of the image. This could be to highlight a menu option from an application, screenshot or a performing artiste, etc.

Look at the pictures in the figure 7.17

Figure: 7.17 (Image Courtesy: StockphotosforFREE.com)

Observe the difference. We have highlighted only a portion of the photo and added a caption. Did we get the desired effect?

More image manipulations

You don't need a fancy DSLR camera or a diploma in photography to add professional-looking photos into your slides.

There are hundreds of photo manipulation and enhancement tools in the market for both Windows and Mac. One very useful and simple tool available online is on http://www.fotor.com/

The following photo has been enhanced with help from the fotor.com website. The website has a plethora of enhancement options that are amazingly simple to do in a jiffy.

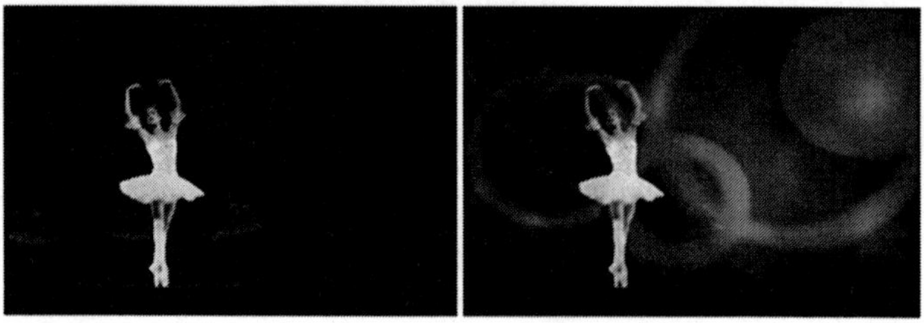

Figure: 7.18 (Image Courtesy: StockphotosforFREE.com)

Photo manipulation is a simple yet effective way to enhance your slides. Explore it.

Geometric shapes

The true power of the creativity, versatility and openness of PowerPoint can be demonstrated with shapes. Shapes offer us a nearly infinite number of possibilities to create interesting visuals.

PowerPoint contains 25 basic shape templates. There are more but we shall ignore similar-looking shapes, and the differences between the various versions of PowerPoint.

For each shape, the following presets and combinations are possible.

- *Over 25 bevel options (top and bottom)*
- *12 surface material effects*
- *15 lighting effects*
- *25 presets for 3D rotation*

Note: There are more possibilities. We are counting only the presets because they can be applied and manipulated in a matter of single/ double clicks.

So, we are talking about various permutations and combinations as follows:

25 shapes x 25 Bevels x 12 Surface Material x 15 Lighting Options x 25 3D Rotation Options.

To illustrate the point, let's look at the following example. In this example, we will see how a simple shape like a square can be converted into a glossy pyramid.

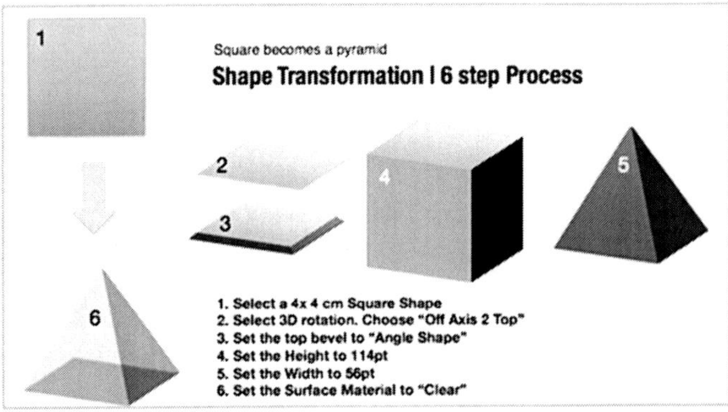

Figure: 7.19 (Image Courtesy: StockphotosforFREE.com)

More shape transformations

We can further manipulate default shapes using an interesting feature called 'edit points'. Select any shape and right click on it to see 'edit points'.

You can convert a triangle into a crown or a beer bottle in a few easy steps. When you have more than two shapes, you can group them together. Once they are grouped, PowerPoint offers yet another useful feature - of deriving a new shape with the following options:

- *Union*
- *Combine*
- *Fragment*
- *Intersect*
- *Subtract*

Microsoft blog gives an apt explanation and a useful illustration using these features. I recommend that you read the article on http://blogs.office.com/2012/03/20/creating-custom-shapes-in-powerpoint-2010

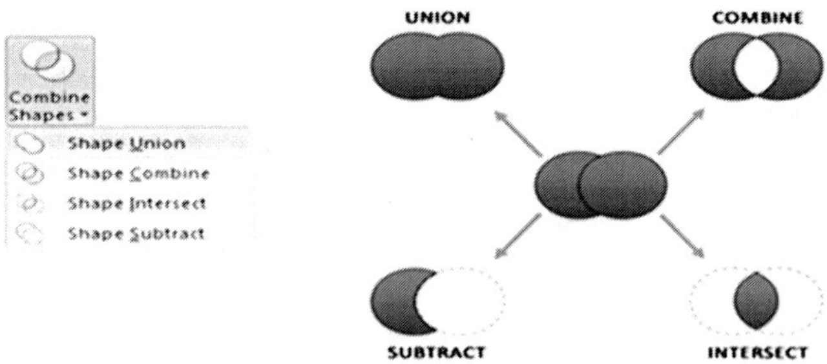

Figure: 7.19 Source: Microsoft Office Blog

Some examples of visuals created using shapes

We have discovered that the current trend in websites and presentations is the flat UI or flat theme. The flat design is minimalistic and is pleasing to the eye. We can use shapes very effectively to create the best flat designs.

Figure: 7.20

Here, the podium effect is created with four rectangular shapes. The middle panel is just a plain rectangle. The side panels are rectangles with basic 3D rotation. The floor panel is yet another rectangle with the corners adjusted to suit the side panels.

The advantages of taking this approach are immense. Firstly, the file size of the presentation will be much smaller as we are not using complex images and photos. They look much better than the actual images; they are free of cost, royalty free and so on.

Putting it all together

We will now create a presentation by applying the concepts of PRISM and SIMPLE.

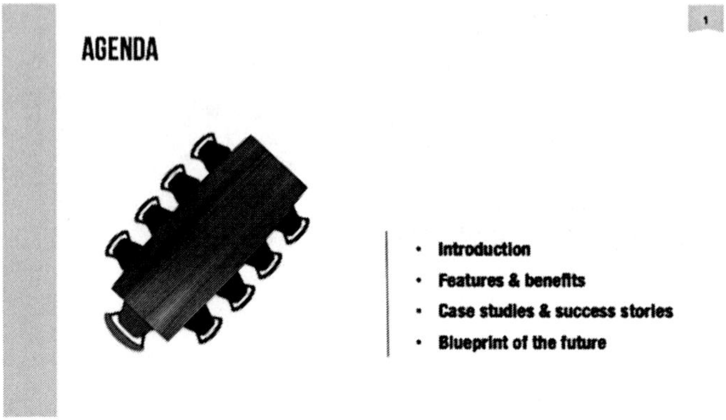
1
AGENDA
Introduction
Features & benefits
Case studies & success stories
Blueprint of the future

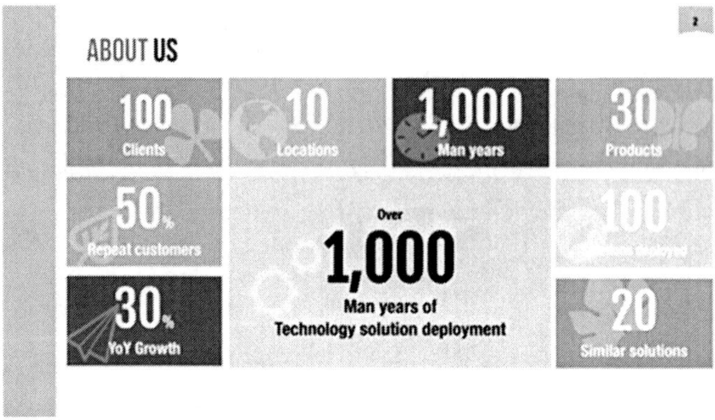
2
ABOUT US
100
Clients
10
Locations
1,000
Man years
30
Products
50%
Repeat customers
Over
1,000
Man years of
Technology solution deployment
100
30%
YoY Growth
20
Similar solutions

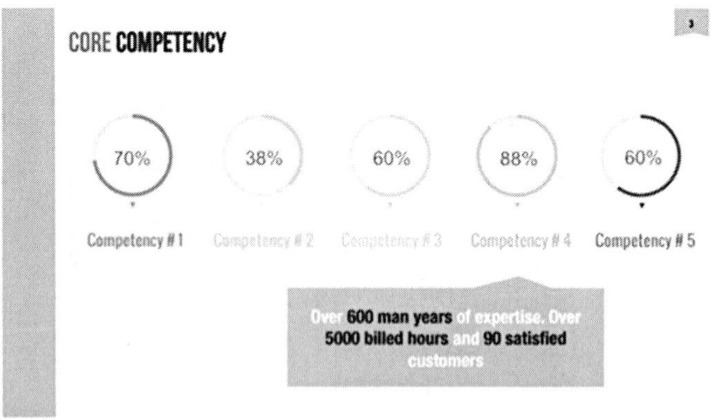
3
CORE COMPETENCY
70%
38%
60%
88%
60%
Competency # 1
Competency # 2
Competency # 3
Competency # 4
Competency # 5
Over 600 man years of expertise. Over 5000 billed hours and 90 satisfied customers

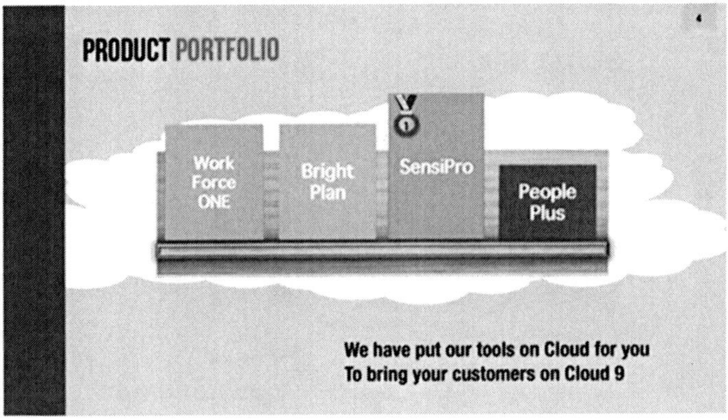
4
PRODUCT PORTFOLIO
Work Force ONE
Bright Plan
SensiPro
People Plus
We have put our tools on Cloud for you
To bring your customers on Cloud 9

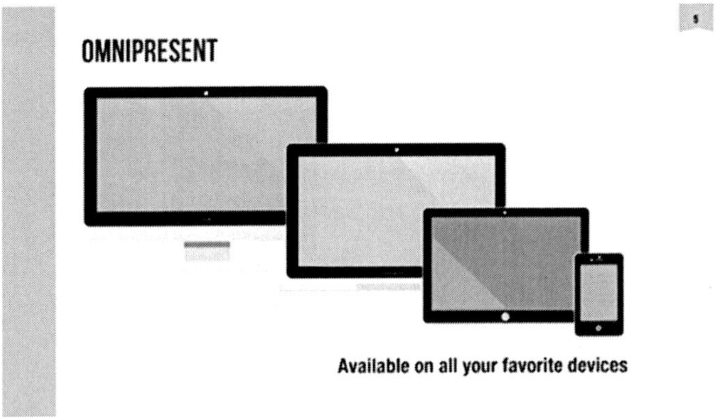
5
OMNIPRESENT
Available on all your favorite devices

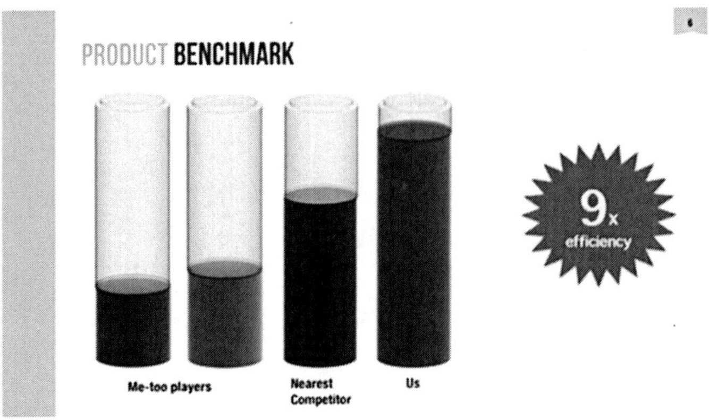
6
PRODUCT BENCHMARK
9x
efficiency
Me-too players
Nearest Competitor
Us

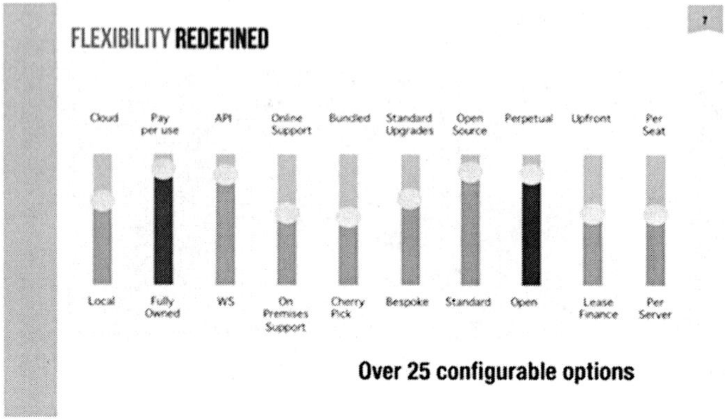
7
FLEXIBILITY REDEFINED
Cloud
Pay per use
API
Online Support
Bundled
Standard Upgrades
Open Source
Perpetual
Upfront
Per Seat
Local
Fully Owned
WS
On Premises Support
Cherry Pick
Bespoke
Standard
Open
Lease Finance
Per Server
Over 25 configurable options

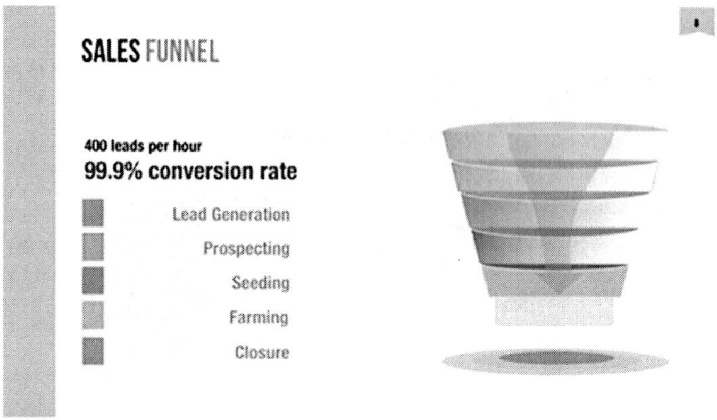
8
SALES FUNNEL
400 leads per hour
99.9% conversion rate
Lead Generation
Prospecting
Seeding
Farming
Closure

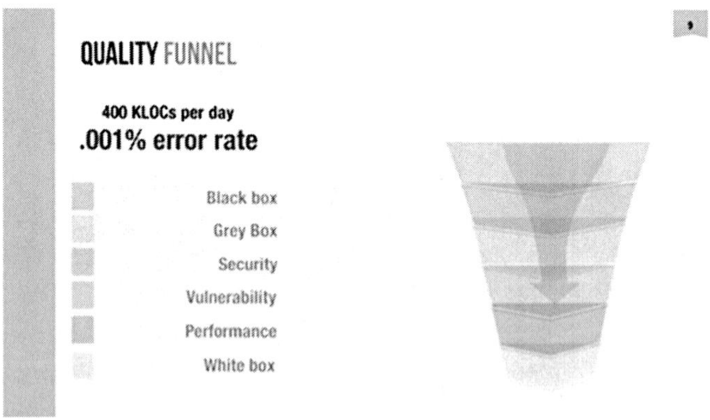
9
QUALITY FUNNEL
400 KLOCs per day
.001% error rate
Black box
Grey Box
Security
Vulnerability
Performance
White box

10

CASE STUDIES

Deal Size ($ '000)	1040	10,200	38,401	800
Team Size	10	15	80	10
Man Months	24	32	84	12
Savings for Client (%)	23	17	50	13
Overall Score	★★★★☆	★★★★★	★★★★★	★★★★☆

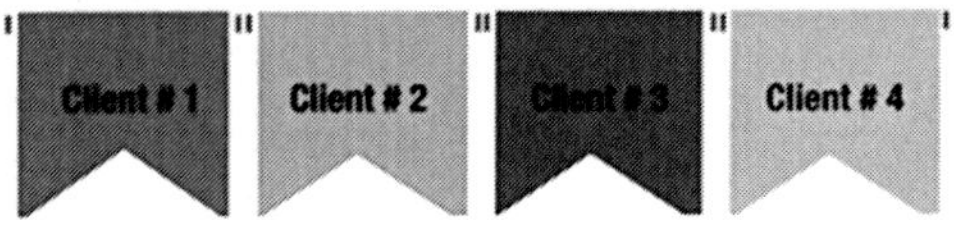

11

RAISING THE BAR

Product	Q1	Q2	Q3	Q4	Overall
WorkForceOne	23.33	22.33	23.89	26.33	▲
BrightPlan	34.34	32.04	31.04	34.34	—
SensiPro	**75.09**	**76.02**	**77.05**	**79.09**	▲
PeoplePlus	21.01	22.03	18.02	17.05	▼

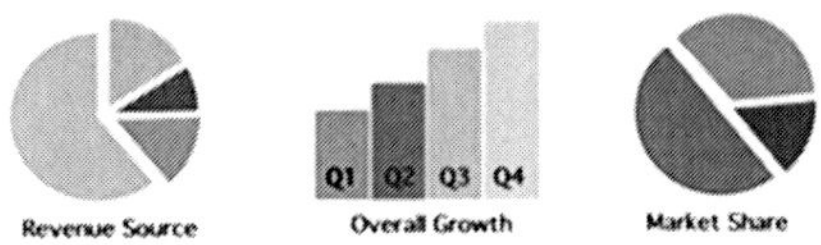

12

GO TO MARKET STRATEGY

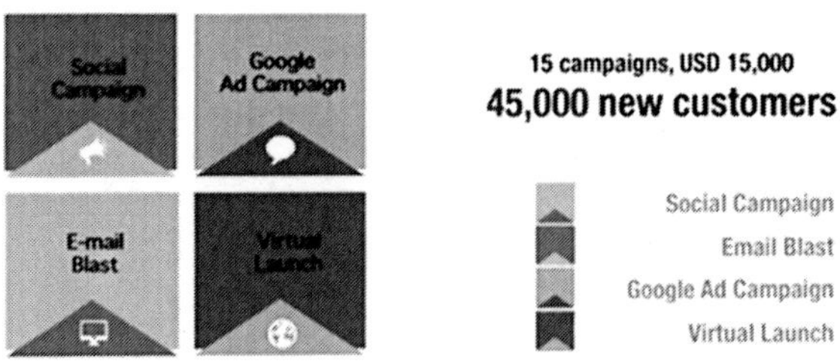

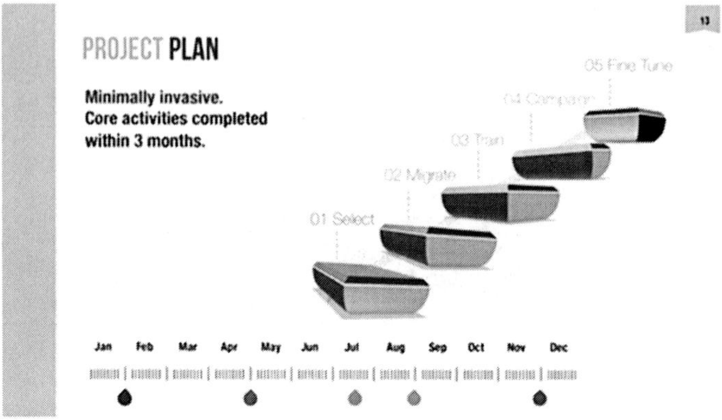
13
PROJECT PLAN
Minimally invasive.
Core activities completed
within 3 months.
05 Fine Tune
02 Migrate
01 Select
Jan Feb Mar Apr May Jun Jul Aug Sep Oct Nov Dec

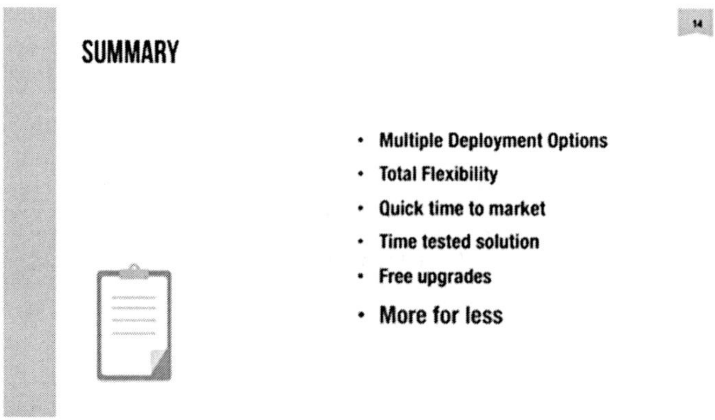
14
SUMMARY
• Multiple Deployment Options
• Total Flexibility
• Quick time to market
• Time tested solution
• Free upgrades
• More for less

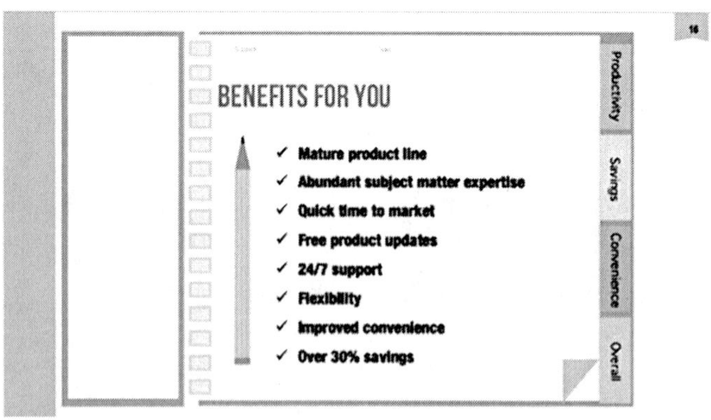
16
BENEFITS FOR YOU
✓ Mature product line
✓ Abundant subject matter expertise
✓ Quick time to market
✓ Free product updates
✓ 24/7 support
✓ Flexibility
✓ Improved convenience
✓ Over 30% savings
Productivity
Savings
Convenience
Overall

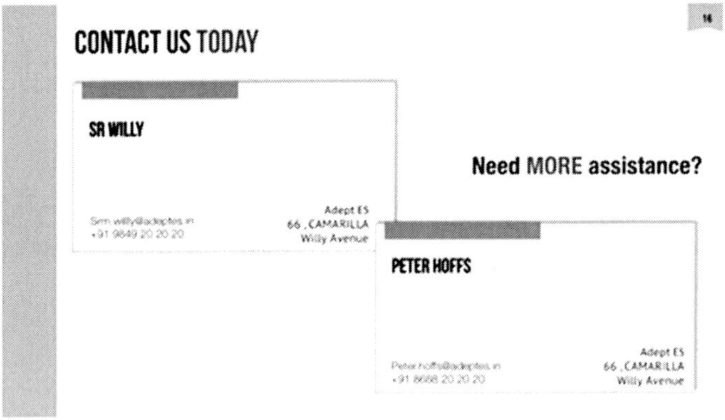

I hope that you would have felt the difference of using PRISM and SIMPLE frameworks.

To showcase the elegance and the simplicity of shapes, I have created the slides using shapes. There are no images/photos or any other external material. Every slide uses only different color and shape options. Please note that the slides can be further enhanced with spice material like quotes, cartoons tag lines and so on. There is also a possibility to add audio and video elements with subtle animation effects. Those additions will further enhance the look and feel of the presentation.

At this stage, I can promise you two things:

- *You won't get into the Guinness Book of Records for packing the maximum information into a single slide*
- *You will not be charged for using more slides in your presentation. So, this is not one of the cost cutting initiatives you need to worry about*

So rest assured, there is no necessity to be stingy with our slides.

This presentation can be downloaded from the site: http://slidespinners.com. You just need to sign up for the newsletter by giving your mail id.

Just go ahead and use this presentation for your needs. This is FREE, hassle free, license free and so on.

I encourage you to give me your feedback and seek support to customize this presentation to suit your requirements.

CHAPTER 8

MODULATION

> "The single biggest problem in communication is the illusion that it has taken place."
>
> - *George Bernard Shaw*

We have so far set the context; fine-tuned the content and presented it in the most appealing manner. What else do we need?

What we need is the mind share -a small place in our prospect's mind to plant a few thoughts. Most importantly, to access the i-Channel.

If this is not done properly, the rest of our efforts will be futile. We then conclude by calling the negative outcome as a "slip between the cup and the lip". But the cup, in reality could be very far.

To bring the cup closer to and to see that our message does not slip and fall through the cracks, we need to do something called Modulation.

To understand this better, let's look at the following scenarios:

1. *You are in a crowded marketplace and suddenly you get a panicked call from someone very important. They are in a crisis situation and you need to give step-by-step instructions, but you can't hear a thing.*
2. *In movies or stories, the heroine is fed wrong information about the hero by another character. She makes his life miserable almost until climax, when finally, the hero clears the air.*
3. *You are trying to explain an important concept to a group of college students. These students are of different intellectual levels. Those who are not able to catch the point are getting bored and distracting the others.*

The communication gap can happen because of a weak signal, noise, a mind that has been corrupted, etc.

Scenario 1

In a crowded market scenario, you tend to emphasize or repeat the important words. This happens unconsciously because of our innate desire to convey the main point. You may eliminate a similar noise in conference rooms but you never know what occupies the listener's mind. You need to identify key messages and make sure that they are modulated in multiple ways. We have done part of this already with fonts, bigger font sizes, colors, shapes, images, etc. But these may not be sufficient to convey some critical messages.

Multimedia (audio and video) as modulation aid

We can use appropriate audio and video clippings to bring about appropriate modulation. Both have a great impact on the overall focus of the subject. According to multi-sensory learning theories, we understand the message by seeing, listening, feeling/touching.

By playing selective audio clips for the important slides, we can maximize the impact. Similarly, a video introduction of a new concept will be very helpful.

Scenario 2

Movie style scenes as described above, surface often in business presentations. It is usual for clients and prospects to attend our sessions with previous 'baggage'. The baggage would have been contributed by a competitor, a disgruntled customer or a disengaged employee. Please recall the points about Blind Spot in chapter 5. It is important to clear the misconceptions and confront the perception upfront.

Scenario 3

This is one of the most frequent and yet most ignored scenarios.

This is a case of one or more of the participants having a negative frame of mind;or he or she is unable to relate to your solution to their problem. The delegate profile sheet should come to our rescue here, but we need to walk that extra mile to reach out to this person.

Many corporates get the psychometric test done for their employees and make it part of their badge. This could provide vital clues about the way they learn, comprehend,relate to and react to various situations.

A detailed explanation about psychometrics is beyond the scope of this book. However, let me state a few examples here:

The Myers Brigs Type Indicator profiles 16 types of personalities, based on the way they react to the following scenarios:

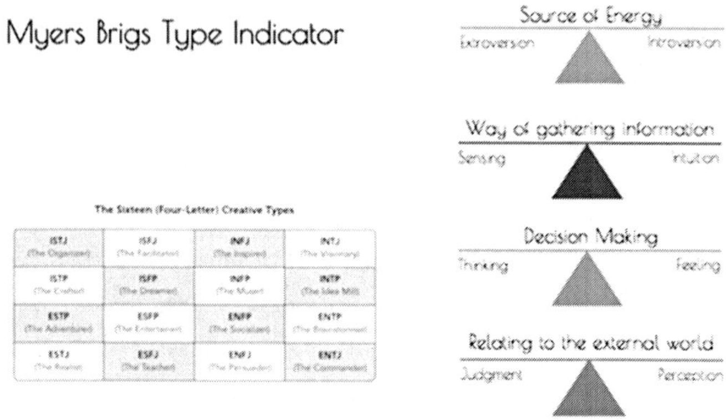

Figure: 8.1

For example, there are people who process information in a sequential flow. They process information by sensing. Another category does not understand anything until the big picture is shown to them. They process information based on intuition.

So, it is essential to modulate our presentation styles to suit these personality types.

Even without any previous baggage or any other distraction, we can unknowingly contribute to the baggage with careless gestures like: a weak handshake, a wrong introduction, etc.

We therefore need to make sure that the appropriate etiquette is followed.

Summary

This brings us to the end of our journey with PRISM. Although I have taken a corporate business pitch scenario, this model can be applicable for a wide variety of presentations.

Compliance to the SIMPLE filter adds an additional flavor to the story.

Like any other skill, presentation development also requires practice and persistence.

So, please go ahead and try to apply these two concepts to your existing presentations. I am confident that you will notice a remarkable improvement.

Section 3

9 CHAPTER

TIPS ON PRESENTATION DELIVERY

> "A smile is a curve that sets everything straight."
>
> *- Phyllis Dille*

As explained in the introductory chapter, this book focuses on presentation development rather than on presentation delivery.

Presentation delivery and public-speaking skills is a vast topic and merits extensive coverage on its own. I hope to cover these in my next book. However, we will discuss the broad contours of presentation delivery in this chapter.

If you adopt the tools, techniques and checklists covered in the last five chapters, you will notice that presentation development is largely oriented towards perfect delivery.

No one is perfect without practice. Look at the most prolific speakers on platforms like TED. For a 20-minute delivery, the speaker would have spent 50 x time rehearsing it.

As Mark Twain points out,"There are two types of speakers. Those who get nervous and those who are liars." If you have to spend

50x time to rehearse to speak the truth, how much time, energy and memory is required to articulate a lie?

Establish common ground with audience before you present. The quickest way to get closer to a person is to explore common interests. Try to find out about your prospects by looking them up on various platforms on the net.

Anticipate questions, objections and be ready with answers. Compile a list of **Rarely Answered Questions** *and find answers to those. You will be glad you did it.*

Always remember that the prospect is not expecting you to be ready with all the answers. You can always, take time and get back to them. If you try to answer everything and if you encounter a question that you cannot answer, you will feel on the back foot.

The prospect's i-channel can forget the numbers, facts and messages. But it will never forget the experience.

Blend the presentation with passion. You will get the right body language naturally, and this in turn, gives a memorable experience for the audience.

What should you wear while making the presentation?

While you have multiple choices in clothing, we have a naturally endowed asset, and that's right on our face.

It is called a Smile.

10 CHAPTER

DISTRIBUTION AND DELIVERY

"Simplicity is the ultimate sophistication."
- Leonardo da Vinci

Great! You have finally created and perhaps even delivered the presentation. It is time to send it to others.

In this chapter, we will look at various options of distributing a presentation and explore the popular tools used for delivering it to remote audiences. We will also look at the recent trends that are likely to change the way that we create presentations in the future.

Distribution

Once you have created the presentation, you may need to send the same to your peers and supervisors for a review. Sometimes, you may even want to send it directly to your clients and prospects. *Converting the presentation to a PowerPoint Show and emailing it is the simplest option.*

In some cases, you may even want to host it on a public platform.

Making the presentation fully public is the easiest option incase you don't have issues of privacy, security and confidentiality with regard to your content.

However, there are some special occasions as listed below:

1. *You want the presentation to be sent to only to a select audience and you want to prevent further sharing.*
2. *You want to track who has seen your presentation so that you can contact them soon after they have watched it.*
3. *You want to analyze the presentation usage and get comments so that you can improve the same.*
4. *The email option is unviable because of the large file size of the presentation and email attachment restrictions.*
5. *You have used some rare fonts which are not available in the destination computer or other devices.*
6. *You want to get the presentation mass printed. You don't want to get into formatting and layout issues with the print service provider.*
7. *Your presentation will be viewed using multiple devices with different screen resolutions.*

In the above scenarios, the standard show and mail option does not work. Let's explore other solutions then.

Portable presentations

Let's assume that you need to send the presentation to your boss for review, or directly to the client. If the fancy fonts that you have used are not available on your boss's computer, then guess what happens? Your boss will take the color out of your life!

PowerPoint offers a facility of saving the slide contents as pictures or video. Video is not a great option to use in this scenario. We will use the 'save as pictures' option. Follow the steps below:

1. *Save and close the presentation*
2. *Open the folder of the presentation*
3. *Copy the original presentation*
4. *Paste it again in the same folder*
5. *Rename the original presentation with the prefix/suffix called Source*
6. *Rename the recent copy of the presentation with the prefix/suffix as Distribution*
7. *You can follow any naming convention. It is okay as long as you have a method to identify the original presentation, and the presentation to be shared or distributed*
8. *Open the distributable version*
9. *Now Click File->Save as -> Pictures -> All Pictures*
10. *Input large values for height and width to suit a high resolution*
11. *Click save*
12. *The dialog box will prompt you to select a folder. Choose one*
13. *Now, PowerPoint saves each slide as slideX.jpg (with x as the slide number)*
14. *Import the slide image into the respective slides*

This may seem like long and laborious work but there are many benefits in this approach.

With this exercise, you have ensured that the content, fonts, formatting and even the colors are protected. These images will look uniform irrespective of the platform used to view it.

However, there are two downsides with this approach:

1. *We will lose all slide level animations because everything is an image*
2. *If the image size is larger, the presentation will take longer to download on a slow network connection*

Note: Page transitions are preserved and can be re-applied.

Since the benefits outnumber the disadvantages, this would be a better way to share a presentation, given the limitations and requirements.

Now choose from the options below to distribute it:

#	Platform	Options	Remarks
1	Browser	Google Slide	
2	Share as Photo album	Picasa or any other photo album sharing option	
3	Public domain	Slideshare	
4	Special Delivery	PointDrive Slideshark.com Slides.com	Invite by mail. Track at every stage Analyze Use remote presentation option Receive comments Make it available on Cloud

Responsive presentations

The numbers of mobile devices (Smart phones, dumb phones, tablets, phablets) is almost competing with numbers of the human population!

Most human beings love to juggle multiple digital devices.

The best way to grab mindshare is through a mobile device. There is no need for concrete proof and complex statistics to emphasize this fact.

How do presentations look and feel on a smart device? Smart or Dumb? Well, if we don't do anything, they will look dumb.

If you have seen some of the best websites, they look equally good on a large desktop or small smart phone. This is achieved by making the website 'Responsive'.

Designers spend considerable time in making sure that the website viewing experience is seamless across devices.

While there are many techniques and tools to bring responsiveness to a website, there is no direct method to achieve the same for a presentation. One of the best options is to create separate versions for desktop and mobile devices.

If you adopt the method of converting the slide contents into images, you are good to go. If not, you may need to rework the presentation to suit the standard resolutions of desktop, tablet and smartphone.

Responsive design is a more responsible design.

Delivery options

Slide broadcast

Microsoft has a native broadcast service to present to a remote audience. This has not become very popular because of a few core limitations. You can still try it and use it. Google search with the key word "PowerPoint broadcast service" - it will give you a link to the Office support site. This site has step-by-step instructions and the latest details.

This service has been introduced slightly ahead of its time and has not been marketed well. I say that it is ahead of time because the release was not synchronized with that of other MS devices like phones, tablets and Xbox consoles. If you have a circle full of Microsoft fans and all of them use Live id and MS devices, you can still give this service a chance.

External tools

There are over a dozen websites/online tools, which rise to the occasion. We will skip the popular sites like Slideshare.com or other popular remote meeting tools like Net meeting, Webex, etc. We will instead look at the following online resources:

1. *Prezi*
2. *PointDrive*
3. *Slides.co*
4. *SlideShark.com*
5. *HTML, CSS and JavaScript Frameworks*

These are explained briefly in Chapter 11.

11 CHAPTER

TREND WATCH

> "Most problems are really the absence of ideas."
> - *PramodBatra*

Microsoft PowerPoint is certainly the most versatile and widely used platform for creating slide presentations. If you are a fan of Google or Apple, you will not be disappointed with their products: Google Slides and Apple Keynote.

However, there are some more good alternatives we should consider. These tools can be very handy when we need to present to larger audiences or showcase some uniqueness.

In addition to the creation capability, we also need a facility to store, share and track our presentation. I have covered those tools as well.

Online/Cloud presentations

If you deliver the presentations in a traditional manner, you save the final presentation on local drives.If it needs to be presented remotely, you use tools like web-ex, remote meeting, etc.

The desire to shift from core competency to further competency is ever increasing. The desire to snatch away our neighbour's job has become order of the day.

With the advent of Cloud services, online presentation creation tools are suddenly on the rise.

Some of these tools do a four-in-one job.

1. *Offer a facility to create presentations*
2. *Provide online storage*
3. *Offer a facility to present it to multiple audiences*
4. *Also offer a comment facility*

These come without any upfront capital expenses. With cost 'variabilization' or pay per use, CFOs have a reason to smile.

While some of them offer run-of-the-mill features, some are innovative and have unique features. The noteworthy tools are as follows:

1. *Prezi.com*
2. *Slide.com*
3. *Slideshark.com*

Prezi.com

Prezi is an online presentation creation and sharing software. It is equipped with an easy-to-use, intuitive tool bar and simple navigation.

Prezi starts with a nice big picture view. Pictures can be zoomed in/zoomed out and panned left or right. The first dozen presentations can give you a thrill and help you flaunt. After that, the eye strain and mental stress makes you go back to the traditional 2D animation effects again!

Slides.com

Slides.com gives us an early preview of future presentations: Slide shows using HTML and CSS. We will cover this shortly.

Slides.com show can be controlled using mobiles/tablets.

Slides.com has integration with Google analytics. That means, you can track who is watching your presentation and from where.

Slideshare.net

Slideshare does not need any separate introduction. Many people are introduced to Slideshare much before they learn to use PowerPoint. It's a great platform and an online community that brings like-minded people together.

Recently, Slideshare.net has introduced the analytics capability also.

Slideshark.com

Slideshark allows standard presentations to be uploaded and shared. It comes with an IOS app. With this, we can control the presentation from an iPhone or an iPad. Slideshark also has the tracking facility enabled.

Voiceboard.co.uk

Everplayed Microsoft Kinect or Playstation Move? Ever thought that a similar capability would be great for presentation delivery too?

Well, the creators of Voiceboard.uk also thought this and brought the concept to reality. It is the Kinect for presentations.

Voiceboard.uk combines voice recognition and gesture control to navigate presentations. It comes with a bluetooth headset and a gesture control ring to achieve voice and motion controls.

VideoScribe.co

This is yet another attempt to take us closer to the I-channel. Videoscribe.co uses a blackboard and scribble effects to illustrate a point.

All you see is a backboard and hands scribbling or drawing something on it, while the background audio explains the concept.

This gives the presentation an impressive look and gets viewer engagement.

VideoScribe is simple to learn and master in a short time. The website offers video tutorials making the learning curve a smooth one.

HTML Presentations - the future of presenting

You must have noticed a significant improvement in the visual appeal of various websites in the last two to three years.

This is thanks to the evolution of rich internet application platforms. Similarly, there has been a significant improvement in the capabilities of HTML, CSS and Javascript.

As I am writing this, HTML5 and CSS 3 are ruling the roost with their versatility. When clubbed with a popular client-scripting language like Javascript, the possibilities become immense. This killer combination gives birth to a whole new concept of script-based presentations on modern browsers.

Because the presentations are available on browsers, there is no dependence on any platform or specific device. Because HTML and CSS are widely used technologies, there is an abundance of talent.

Since this is on a browser, integration or inter-operability with other internet applications or audio/video files becomes simple.

To make life simpler, there are over a dozen presentation frameworks in the market today. Popular among those are: Desk.js, impress.js and reveal.js.

The Slides.com site referred to in the previous section, uses one such framework.

If you are familiar with web development, I strongly recommend that you try these.

Browser support in PowerPoint

PowerPoint offers a facility to embed a browser within the slides. This feature is not well-known but is a very powerful feature if used in the right manner. Browser support is handy in the following situations:

1. We need to give a *product demo which is browser based*
2. *We need to switch between the slideshow and the browser (for website, Facebook, Twitter or similar platforms)*
3. *The presentation has hyperlinks to various online resources*

There are multiple ways of embedding a browser. If you know a bit of coding, the browser can be placed directly on the slide and controlled programatically.

There is a third party tool called Live Web:http://skp.mvps.org/liveweb.htm#.VKCs1BOs

If you are not familiar with web development, this is probably a good time to start learning it.

Note: Browser control requires macro permissions and knowledge of programming. Use it with discretion.

Summary

The objective of mentioning these tools is merely to give you an idea about the various trends that are current and equip you with the knowledge of how to use them best.

All these tools belong to separate categories and have their own strengths and shortcomings. We need to weigh these based on the need of the hour. I recommend that you visit these sites and watch the respective intro videos and showcase presentations. It will be an educative session.

If you want to see a detailed comparison, there is yet another site: www.itqlick.com. This website gives detailed reviews of various software products and has very pleasing UI. Needless to mention, there are numerous blogs as well. However, I personally find the comparison of these products a bit unequal, because it cannot be an apple-to-apple comparison. These tools belong to different categories, and are based on different parameters like pricing and capabilities. While some of them are free, some are fully paid or pay per use.

On the capability/features front, some are used for presentation creation while some of them are useful only for broadcasting, with limited or no capabilities for editing.

You can consider the following combinations:

For a business pitch presentation that needs to be sent to a select audience with tracking requirements, use Point Drive with PowerPoint Slide Images.

For a presentation that you want to share within your circles and closed user groups, use Google slides with PowerPoint Slide Images.

If you want to give a short and flashy demo, consider Prezi.

If you have full resources (time, money, people who can support) and a strong cause to do something out-of-the-box, consider VideoScribe.

If you are very creative/innovative and have found a better combination or a tool, share the idea with me!

Privacy and confidentiality.

Like any other trend, Cloud platform and technology are getting being glorified without an eye on the basic hygiene factors. Presentations can contain private/ confidential information. With more and more security lapses and large enterprises falling prey to cyber attacks, the safety of Cloud presentations remains a question mark.

12 CHAPTER

SEEING BEYOND

> "It's not what you look at that matters, it's what you see."
>
> *- Henry David Thoreau*

With this chapter, we have come to the end of our journey to demystify the presentation. By now, you should be familiar with the various aspects of structured presentation development and suitable deployment options.

However, you may still wonder: "Will I be able to independently develop presentations?"

This is a common question that haunts everyone who is new to presentations.

In this chapter, we will look at how we can explore the hidden talent required for creating presentations. We will also understand a method to identify this talent within the people around us.

We will also explore various online resources to help us with presentation development. These resources will be extremely helpful in greatly simplifying the presentation development process and also in enhancing the quality of the presentation.

Converting the potential to flair

Finding the power within.

I have mentioned in the earlier chapter that creativity is a skill and that it can be nurtured and developed further. You need to surf your inner-net to find if you do have a flair for creating presentations. How do you discovery our hidden potential?

Let's assume that you are constructing a home in an open land. One of the first things that you need to do is to dig a bore well,to ensure that you have adequate supply of water for construction and also for future use. But you cannot find the hidden water sources on your own. You have to call a ground water expert and let him run few tests to explore the potential sources of water. You will then get the bore well dug in the prescribed spot – with chances of maximum success. You will then refine or purify the water and make it potable.

Talent mining is no different from water mining. You need to get the expert (in this case, the talent diviner) to explore your hidden potential. You need to take the effort to dig deeper to develop the skill. You need to practice and refine it further until it becomes an established talent.

The question is: Who will do the talent mining? The answer is: psychometric tools.

It is a good idea to take personality evaluation tools like enneagram, MBTI and strength finder.

While we nurture our creative skills, it is also important to spot a person in our team who shows an ability to create presentations. Let's take an example here. One of the easiest ways to identify the person is to let the entire team take the strengthfinder.com test. It is online, accurate and the report comes to you instantly. There are certain signature themes that offer pointers to our search and you can start from there.

Assuming that you are able to find one or two members in your team who have the highest potential for creativity, you can 'in-source' this activity to them by freeing them up, changing their roles or by motivating them suitably. You will then accomplish two things. Get up to the speed with the market demands and piggyback on them to learn the techniques they master from time to time.

On the other hand, there are some inherent personality indicators that show ability for such flair. I list them below:

- *I organize my desk at the workplace*
- *I understand the importance of dressing up suitably for every occasion*
- *I don't like to read unformatted text, poorly framed sentences*
- *I am a stickler for perfection*
- *People usually find bullet points and numbered lists in anything that I write*

Postmortem: Look at your old presentations and see how many slides comply with our checklist.

Pick a subject of your choice or interest and create a presentation that explains the concepts to a layman. If you are a financial advisor, try and explain the concept of investments via a presentation. If you are a physics teacher, explain the law of gravity. If you like cars, explain what Torque and Power are.

Adobe, since its inception, is known for its creative tools and ideas. These tools have helped many creative people flourish and make their passion their profession. Now Adobe has taken yet another initiative to nurture creative talent: behance.net. This is an excellent platform for creative professionals to share their work, get recognized and in turn, find opportunities. There an affiliate platform called http://99u.com *that offers various insights on creativity. 99u.com for creative professionals is what TED.com is to leadership professionals. You can get plenty of inspiration for your creativity here.*

Also browse the following sites for your daily/weekly dose of creativity:

http://doublemesh.com

http://every-tuesday.com

https://www.behance.net

You are not alone

Stuck with something? Still not equipped with the required capabilities? Don't know how to create that stunning visual? Got the idea but don't have time?

While developing presentations, it is usual to get stuck and feel helpless.

The problems that we face are not unique to us. There are thousands of professionals who are staring at such deadlocks.

Well, fortunately, we are in a very connected world - there are hundreds of experts waiting to help us with many online tools and sites. Let's explore some of these now.

For graphics, images, footage and illustrations:

- *Envato.net*
- *Shutterstock.com*
- *Fotolia.com*

For presentation themes, graphics, animations, etc.:

- *PresentationProcess.com*
- *PresenterMedia.com*
- *PresentationModel.com*

For animations and video:

- *Videoscribe.com*
- *Powtoon.com*
- *Wideo.co*
- *Moovly.com*

For infographics

- *Piktochart.com*
- *Visual.ly*
- *Pinterest.com*

For rapid prototyping of software applications:

- Keynotopia.com

For images:

- *Commoncraft.com*

For freelancer talent/resources:

- *Elance.com*
- *oDesk.com*
- *Freelancer.com*
- *Google Helpout*

For learning and development:

- *Pluralsight.com is on a rapid expansion spree and is acquiring companies with powerful credentials*
- *Lynda.com*

Daily Prayer: God, give me enough creativity to develop great visuals or fund me enough to afford those I cannot develop.

To sum up, in this Information Age, when the world is digital, you are never alone. There are several genies waiting to help you.

You can also feel free to reach me anytime for support or guidance. Please register yourself at the website Slidespinners.com and explore various online resources there.

Wish you good luck!

ANNEXURE 1

PRE-FINISH CHECKLIST

> **"By three methods we may learn wisdom: First, by reflection, which is noblest; Second, by imitation, which is easiest; and third by experience, which is the bitterest."**
>
> *- Confucius*

Here are the two types of checklists that you can use:

Routine checklist

- ☑ *I know the intent of the presentation*
- ☑ *I have packaged what the audience want to see and not what I know*
- ☑ *I have started with the end in mind*
- ☑ *The presentation has a story with a Hero and a Villain*
- ☑ *I have understood the audience profile*
- ☑ *Each slide has passed the SIMPLE test*
- ☑ *The presentation does not look like a documentary*
- ☑ *I have used pictures,info-graphics and statistics effectively*
- ☑ *I have packed enough evidence in the slides to create trust and credibility*
- ☑ *The presentation is visually appealing*

This is a long checklist. Here is a shorter and smarter version for you:

Smart checklist

☑ *I have read the SlideSpin book completely*

☑ *I have ensured that the people who are involved in the presentation have also read this book*

☑ *I have used the PRISM framework*

☑ *All slides have passed the SIMPLE test*

ANNEXURE 2

USEFUL ONLINE RESOURCES

Graphics, images and illustrations

Envato.net

Fotolia.com

Shutterstock.com

Stockvault.net

freerangestock.com

openphoto.net

StockphotosforFREE.com

Presentation elements

PresenterMedia.com

PresentationProcess.com

PresentationModel.com

Animations, video effects

Powtoon.com

Videoscribe.com

wideo.co

moovly.com

Prezi.com

Visual.ly

Pinterest.com

Keynotopia.com

Commoncraft.com

Talent for presentations, creative design and more

Elance.com

oDesk.com

Freelancer.com

Google Helpout

Knowledge, self-paced learning and development

Pluralsight.com

Lynda.com

Color

www.colorcombos.com

http://colorschemedesigner.com

http://www.colorhunter.com/.

Image adjustment

http://www.pictaculous.com/

http://www.fotor.com

Others

http://fontawesome.io/

http://thephilosophicalboy.files.wordpress.com

http://skp.mvps.org/liveweb.htm#.VKCs1BOs

www.itqlick.com

http://99u.com

BIBLIOGRAPHY

Word Salad - Wikipedia: The Free Encyclopedia. Wikimedia Foundation, Inc., date last updated (16 November 2014 at 20:53). Web. Date accessed (16 December 2014).<http://en.wikipedia.org/wiki/Word_salad>

Thomas Fuller - BrainyQuote.com. Xplore Inc, 2014. 25 December 2014.

http://www.brainyquote.com/quotes/quotes/t/thomasfull125402.html

DISCLAIMER

The information provided within this book is for general informational purposes only. While we try to keep the information up-to-date and correct, there are no representations or warranties, express or implied, about the completeness, accuracy, reliability, suitability or availability with respect to the information, products, services, or related graphics contained in this book for any purpose. Any use of this information is at your own risk.

The methods described within this book are the author's personal thoughts and illustration only, without warranty either expressed or implied. They are not intended to be a definitive set of instructions. You may discover there are other methods and materials to accomplish the same end result.

INDEX

ABOUT AUTHOR

SuRa is a technology management professional with in depth knowledge of enterprise application and team integration. He has expertise in people and process alignment, business transformation and strategic IT management.

He has more than 20 years of experience across various facets of IT vizapplication architecture, network architecture, security, User Interface design, etc.,

Sura is Slide Spinner with over 12,000 hours on creating corporate presentations and training professionals on presentation skills.

He is currently working as an Executive Director at Karvy Insurance Repository.

He can be reached at sr@slidespinners.com

Thank You For Your Time

Thank you for your time. Hope you have enjoyed reading the Slide Spin book and found it useful. I recommend you to download the companion work book also. Slide Spin Personal Work Book is full of exercises, practical examples, assessments and so on.

I truly value your feedback to develop the book further. I would be grateful if you can take out few minutes to leave a review on Amazon.com.

You can also download a ready to use presentation template from my website. Visit www.SlideSpinners.Com/Club for more details.

Yours truly,

Subbarao Mukkavilli